TRANSGRESSIVE CIRCULATION

ESSAYS ON TRANSLATION

johannes göransson

D1715054

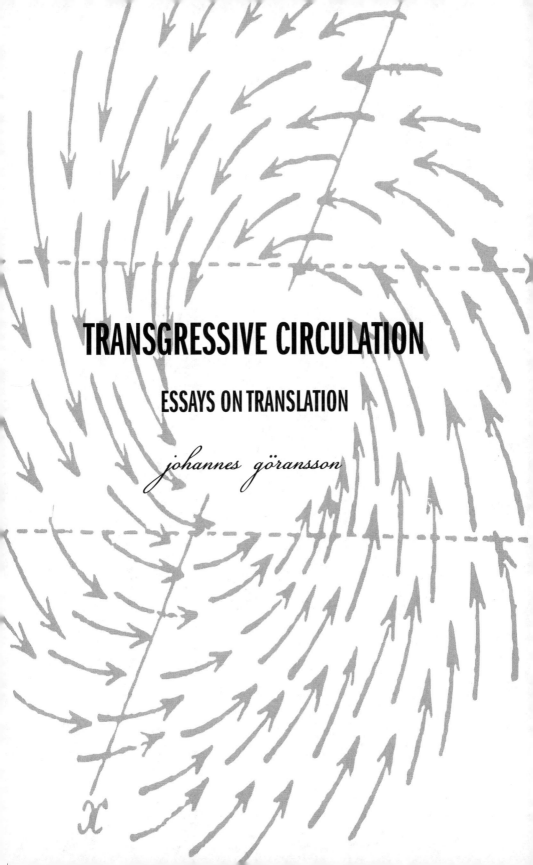

TRANSGRESSIVE CIRCULATION

ESSAYS ON TRANSLATION

johannes göransson

Book Cover Design: Steve Halle
Book Interior Design: Sarah Gzemski

Published by Noemi Press, Inc. A Nonprofit Literary Organization.
www.noemipress.org.

Contents

1

INTRODUCTION: THE DEFORMATION ZONE OF TRANSLATION

1.

Perhaps the most durable (and quotable) definition of poetry in modern US literature is Robert Frost's quip that "poetry is what is lost in translation." As in so many discussions about poetry over the past two hundred years, poetry here is defined as the un-translatable; poetry as an essence of authenticity. As in so many discussions about the *translation* of poetry, translation becomes poetry's opposite: inauthentic, mediated, fake, a version, a bad copy, counterfeit. The essence of the poem can only be found in its originality; in versioning, this is lost. One might translate the words, but not the poem's originality, interiority, or authenticity.

When Frost defines translation as the negation of poetry, he makes poetry vulnerable to translation. Translation undoes some essence that gives a poem its "poetry." Poetry and translation are caught in a volatile relationship. This relationship has a name: "Impossible." In the discussions surrounding translation and poetry since the late 18th century, few words or ideas reoccur with such persistence as the word "impossibility." Translating poetry is impossible because it challenges entrenched ideas about authorship, poem and context.

This is a book about this impossible relationship. I'm interested in the dynamics of translation that so frequently renders it into a kind of abject of poetry. I will not solve this impossibility, but I will argue that the impossibility of translation participates in and foregrounds a volatile dynamic that is central to poetry: transgressive circulation.

2.

The idea of translation's impossibility is peculiar since we know that poetry is translated all the time. Although the US literary establishment has a history of marginalizing, stabilizing and containing foreign literature in translation, there are many examples of foreign literature having profound effects on US literature. The most obvious example may be Ezra Pound who used his translations of Chinese poetry to develop a new branch of US modernism. Another example, perhaps as obvious and perhaps as influential, is the translation of poets like Tomas Tranströmer, Federico García Lorca and Pablo Neruda in the 1950s and 1960s by poets like Robert Bly and Clayton Eshleman. These translations helped – at least for a few years –challenge the ideals and rules of the New Critical establishment in US poetry and give rise to a less US-centric idea of poetry. But even outside of these instances of international attention and influence, translators have been translating poetry throughout the twentieth century. How can their act be seen as impossible when it so clearly happens all the time? This question may seem facetious but it hides a proliferation of other questions: What is the true purpose of claiming (or acting as if) poetry cannot be translated? What models of poetry does it establish? What models of lineage and literary history? What models of reading poetry does it perpetuate? What is the purpose of such a limited and limiting definition of poetry? Why is poetry so vulnerable to translation? What makes poetry impossible to translate?

To begin answering these questions, we might ask what is – on a very obvious level – "lost" in translation?

The short answer is the paradigm of the un-paraphraseable text, written by a single author, operating as part of a national lineage. The ideal of the poem as unparaphraseable is one of the most pervasive rules in modern discussions of US poetry: any version of the poem is inherently a degradation because every word is in the right place. The poet's authority assures the reader that the poem is not accidental, not noise. It guarantees the text's value. Translation displaces the poem from the originator, the master, introducing the possibility of noise in the versioning of the translation. The reader loses the assurance – or "currency" – of mastery, opening up the threat that the poem might be a hoax, a counterfeit. The threat of translation is the threat of excess: too many versions of too many texts by too many authors from too many lineages. Poetry becomes too volatile in translation's excess.

3.

In this excess of translation, we are not masters; we are as much mastered by the art as we master it. Rather than the common American ideal of "accessible" (or "difficult") poetry, we should see the act of reading as making ourselves accessible to poetry, to its transgressive circulation. I might borrow a phrase from the visual arts: the art critic Renée Hoogland insightfully writes that to engage with an artwork – to have an aesthetic "encounter" – means to "open oneself up to its potentially deregulating power. Embracing a work of art is being embraced by it."[1] *Transgressive Circulation* argues that poetry – and especially poetry in translation – gives its readers this "violent embrace."

It is this "deregulating" "embrace" that Joyelle McSweeney and I aimed to describe in our booklet *Deformation Zone*.[2] Poet and translator, "original" and translation: all participate in a deformation zone in which the counterfeit infects the original, the original "context," and the target culture, opening up a "deregulating" space of poetic "encounters." This volatile zone challenges the illusion of a linear, patriarchal lineage, and with it, the objectivity of that lineage: Who is considered a good poet? Who is influencing who? What if a writer is influenced by a text that is alien to her? Can she really be influenced correctly? Is she misreading it? But perhaps most of all, it challenges the very idea of the poem as something that we access whether it is "accessible" or "difficult". The deformation zone questions this model of agency. It foregrounds the way our relationship as readers and writers is far more volatile than in the traditional model of reader-as-accessor of the poem.

McSweeney and I took the term "deformation zone" from my translation of the Swedish poet Aase Berg's poem "Deformationszon," from her book *Uppland*. The book depicts a family idyll and simultaneously a plane crash that never happens. The family and the plane vibrate between flying and crashing, instead turning into "dragonflies," via a Swedish-English pun that proliferates and co-morbidly infects and is infected by both languages. For example, she mistranslates "dragonfly" as "drakfly" ("dragonflee") instead of the standard term "trollslända." The English becomes a foreign substance entering the Swedish language, which in turn breaks down the Swedish word "trollslända": One might say she creates a line of flight for the "slända," a word that can mean both the taxonomic group of the "dragonfly" and the textile term "spindle" ("troll" in turn means something like "enchant"). Instead of separate languages, Swedish and

[1]Renée Hoogland, *A Violent Embrace* (Hanover, NH: Dartmouth College Press, 2014), 2.

[2]Joyelle McSweeney and Johannes Göransson, *Deformation Zone* (New York: Ugly Duckling Presse, 2012).

English become involved in a "violent embrace." The "deformation zone" of Berg's poem is a volatile space that vibrates between crashing and flying to "Ängland" – which means "Meadowland" semantically, but which of course is a homophonic pun on "England" – between Swedish and English, between the privacy of the family and the public space of the Swedish welfare state increasingly contested by forces of globalization.

Berg takes the term from meteorology where a "deformation zone is a region of significant stretching in the atmosphere. The stretching is often caused by airstreams flowing toward each other and then fanning out as they meet."[3] As in meteorology, the poem is a volatile zone of interaction. The transgressive circulation occasioned by the translation-as-poem engages with linguistic and cultural boundaries. It doesn't transcend them, but involves them in a "violent" and potentially "deregulating" embrace.

4.

The noisy, violent excess of translation ruins the illusion of monoglossic completion and isolation. It makes us uncertain, opens us to the weirdness of art; it takes away the handles, the guard rails, the control; it asks us to engage with the intensive strangeness of art intensively; it asks us to bring the far-away up close, to see the close-by as strange. It makes us uncanny readers of poetry: what is domestic becomes foreign, the foreign domestic. Translation questions the very idea of a nationally coherent literature, opening up multiplicity within the supposed linguistic boundaries of the national literature. The foreign exists within and across these boundaries.

While there is a desire to maintain boundaries, there is also a great pleasure in flooding borders, troubling boundaries, contaminating systems. Drawing on George Bataille's idea of art as excess, Daniel Tiffany notes, that "[t]he 'accursed share' produces pleasure, though it is founded on a logic of prohibition by swallowing the other, by contaminating itself and traversing its own boundaries."[4] This book is also about this contaminatory, "accursed" logic. In contrast to the pervasive models where the morality, ethics and politics of poetry are invested in a tasteful and pedagogical distancing, this book advocates its opposite: an immersion in the text, in the "too-much-ness" of poetry, in the unhierarchized, unredeemed art. I advocate bringing the abject back into plain view. I advocate art's violent embrace.

---

[3]National Weather Service, *Deformation Zones*. http://www.crh.noaa.gov/Image/lmk/pdf/deformation_zones.pdf .
[4]Daniel Tiffany, *Radio Corpse: Imagism and the Cryptaesthetic of Ezra Pound* (Cambridge: Harvard U.P., 1998), 161.

5.

Translation discussions are often contradictory and I am not immune to contradictions. Translation is, as Lawrence Venuti has put it, a "scandal." Venuti has his own solution to this issue: making the translator and the translation visible by foregrounding the translatedness of the text, thus establishing a pedagogical, critical distance. My own approach is somewhat different. I want to use its scandal to reconfigure not just how we do or don't read translation, but how we read poetry as a whole. If the constant urge to quarantine this scandal has in many ways defined poetry for the past two hundred years, I don't want to remove the scandal, I want to inhabit it. I want to find out what rat is buried in this scandal and I want to see how digging it up might change the way we read poetry. I want to dwell in translation's abject zone, not just to read works in translation but also to read US poetry through this scandalous, corrupting framework.

I am not advocating a hygienic, utopian vision of poetry without borders. Translation – like art itself – tends to amplify issues of power and conflict. Rejecting translation because of such political problems is just another way to preserve a privileged monoglossia. But I am not trying to sweep such issues under the carpet; rather, I want to include as much of it in the book as I can. The transgressive circulation of translations tends to foreground thorny issues, troubling histories. That is part of the reason we have to investigate the abjection of US literary culture; our literary culture has been too hygienic and clean, too eager to make itself unproblematic and edifying, for too long.

This book is about the noisy, violent excess of translation and poetry, but it is also about the rhetoric used to abject this excess (for example, the insistent use of anti-kitsch rhetoric). This book is about the body, movement and art. It's about sensations. It's about uncertainty and repulsion. It's about hatred. It's about the night of art. But most of all it is about exploring an "impossibility" that, rather than prohibit, can open up dynamic, strange zones of experience.

If the US definition of poetry excludes translation, it might be that we need to alter that definition. It might be that this ideal for poetry is meant to maintain a monoglossic and nationalistic model of poetry, and to exclude the transgressive movements and transformations that translation generates. It might not be that we need to constantly wring our hands over the methods of translating, but rather that we need to pay attention to the failures of translation and through them open up our ideas of poetry, culture and authorship. Taking a cue from Judith Halberstam, we might say that translation offers a "queer art of failure" that challenges the inherent conservatism of our literary ideals. In its failure to be poetry, translation generates a proliferation that undermines the illusion of economic stability perpetuated by nation-based models of translation. This does not mean that it is the opposite of poetry. Instead of focusing all discussion about translation on "losses" and "gains" – economic paradigms meant to maintain normalcy and stability – I will argue that this proliferation is an exciting space for poetry, a space of movement, invention, deformation and transgressive circulation.

6.

In the continual attempts to control the transgressive circulation enacted by translation, I see not just an anxiety about translation, but an anxiety about poetry, writing, art. Rather than the antithesis of poetry, translation foregrounds something essential about poetry: the way it is spread, the way it moves, the way it invites imitations and deformations and thereby disrupts hierarchies. Therefore, when I write about translation, I am writing about art. This book has its origins in discussions about translation but its aim is not a methodology of translation. Instead it assumes translation is the epitome of poetry and art, and its attempt to trace translation's lawless ways is an attempt to theorize poetry and art.

2

"TRANSGRESSIVE CIRCULATION": COMMUNICATION AND EXCESS

1.

The relationship between poetry and translation is defined in part by the relationship between the ideal of communication and the threat of "communication failure" that John Durham Peters discusses in his book *Speaking Into the Air: A History of the Idea of Communication*. Peters argues that Western society (especially since the nineteenth century but as early as the Greeks) has developed both an ideal of "communication" as an act of "direct contact between interiorities" as well as an interdependent anxiety about the threat of "communication failure." Peters argues that the ideal of "communication" and the anxiety about the threat of "communication failure" are inseparable and simultaneous:

> "Communication is a homeopathic remedy: the disease and the cure are in cahoots. It is a compensatory ideal whose force depends on its contrast with failure and breakdown. Miscommunication is the scandal that motivates the very concept of communication in the first place."[5]

"Communication failure" both threatens ideal communication and justifies that ideal. The threat derives from the sense that communicating one's interiority inherently creates a risk of corruption. In order to communicate one's interiority, one must translate it, but that very act makes one's interiority vulnerable to deformation and miscommunication. According to Peters, the influence of this troubled relationship has grown ever more

---

[5]John Durham Peters, Speaking Into the Air: A History of the Idea of Communication (Chicago: University of Chicago Press, 2001), 6.

pervasive in the modern age, as a direct response to the sense of modern mass media as distracting, sensationalistic and overwhelming.

In describing the communication paradigm, Peters explores the historical development of the ideal of communication, from Plato and Socrates up through industrialization to the current era, in which authentic communication is increasingly posited as an antidote to the overwhelming influence of mass communication. Peters notes that in Plato's *Phaedrus*, Socrates condemns writing for being sensationalistic in its spreading of rhetoric outside the immediacy of the direct relationship of dialogues, into foreign areas where the readers may misunderstand the text:

> "The mis-en-scène of the dialogue thus sketches the theme of the transgressive circulation of the written word, its ability to wander beyond the original context of its oral, interactive presence, just as Phaedrus and Socrates circulate outside the bounds of the city."[6]

Written language becomes a source of confusion precisely because of its "transgressive circulation": writing is dangerous because it puts a work into circulation, opening it up to misinterpretation. Already in 370 BC, discussions about communication and writing evidence a fundamental anxiety about excess which maps onto our contemporary anxiety about translation: there will be too many versions of the text, in too many places, with too many readers, from places that are too far away.

Socrates is not just worried that the "transgressive circulation" of writing will lead to misinterpretation. He is also anxious that it will make readers vulnerable to dangers involving the power and erotics of (what I will call) "foreign influence." Socrates believes writing will lead to a power imbalance because to read a text – to put a foreign text in one's mouth, and thus one's body – is akin to being controlled by a foreign writer. Peters paraphrases Socrates's views thus: "To read - which meant to read aloud – was to relinquish control of one's body to the (masculine) writer, to yield to a distant dominating body."[7] Speaking to a person you know (someone from inside Athens) "face-to-face," for Socrates, was a democratic ideal. Reading any writer (but especially a foreign writer) and taking that writer's words inside your body was akin to being sodomized, to losing one's sovereignty, one's autonomy. "Transgressive circulation" threatens hierarchies by activating the erotic anxiety which power seeks to control.

---

[6]Ibid., 38.
[7]Ibid., 40.

2.

According to Peters, these anxieties about transgressive circulation, un-faithful dissemination and inflation reach a greater intensity in the modern age with the proliferation of various technologies that quickly and widely disseminate more material, faster, to more distant places. It is here that Peters finds the true birth of the model of "communication" that he analyzes: "Putting it too starkly, in the 1830s and 1840s the photograph overcame time and the telegraph overcame space."[8] As the reach of media grew, the anxieties of non-dialogic communication became even more intensive. Human faces, bodies and voices were circulated – but what they lacked was their humanness, their interiority. It was the person, but it also wasn't the person. They were ghost-like. Peters quotes Friedrich Kittler: "Media always already yield ghost phenomena."[9]

Anxiety about mass-communicated propaganda and advertisements – messages meant to spread to as many people as possible, indiscriminately – has generated a greater urge for unmediated, authentic expression. The handwringing about mass dissemination results in the increased emphasis on – and anxiety about the loss of – "privacy": "privacy, quite explicitly, emerges as a concern once it is threatened by new media of image and sound recording."[10] Discussing the invention of the telephone, Peters writes: "the telephone evoked many of the same anxieties as radio: strange voices entering the home, forced encounters, the disappearance of one's words into an empty black hole, and absent faces of the listeners."[11] Modern media manifests as an anxiety about "strangeness" – foreign presence that invades bourgeois privacy, domesticity. From that time to the present, an influential faction of communication theorists has criticized modern media both for its lack (its ability to generate apparitions, bodiless, lacking both faces and interiority) and its too-much-ness (its proliferous invasion of the domestic sphere). The same anxieties and threats of excess, sensationalism and circulation have a defining influence on US poetry - especially the poetry of what Mark McGurl has called "the program era" – and has resulted in its conservative approach toward translation.

3.

The close connection between the idealization of communication and Anglo-American literature is not accidental: Many of the primary proponents

---

[8]Ibid., 140.
[9]Ibid., 140.
[10]Ibid., 174.
[11]Ibid., 198.

of the communication ideal were literary critics who believed that literature could serve the function of idealized communication in an age of noisy mass communication. One of the key modern proponents of the importance of communication was British philosopher and educator I.A. Richards, the scholar who began the New Critical project which completely transformed the US practice of teaching and reading poetry, and which— as described by McGurl in *The Program Era* — served as a major influence on the creation of the MFA workshop. In his book *Practical Criticism*, Richards argues:

> "The whole apparatus of critical rules and principles is a means to the attainment of fine, more precise, more discriminating communication... When we have solved, completely, the communication problem, when we have got, perfectly, the experience, the mental condition relevant to the poem, we still have to judge it, still to decide upon its worth."[12]

Richards based his aesthetics on a pedagogical model that focused on the communication of interiorities, or as Peters puts it, the "accurate sharing of consciousness."[13] What assures communication depends on readers having learned to read properly ("close reading"), which allows them to access the meaning of the poem, and to be "discriminating," thus able to determine the poem's "worth." In the end, the New Critical paradigm - like the communication ideal – functions according to an economic principle: meaning is the gold standard ensuring the value of language, while language is a currency otherwise susceptible to nonsense, inflation, chaos.[14]

For Richards, the ideal of communication had two main enemies: "the impasse of solipsism" and the "veritable orgy of verbomania."[15] He believed these threats could be countered with an aesthetics of moderation and a model of reading which "accesses" the interiority of poems. Richards's fear of an "orgy" that floods the reader has had large consequences for both the "workshop" aesthetic and US discussions about translation. The key to good poetry becomes a matter of learning how to become discriminating, how to filter out the too-much-ness of "verbomania."

Perhaps surprisingly, Richards did not see a problem with translation. As Edwin Gentzler discusses in *Contemporary Translation Theories*, Richards's views on translation – like his views on poetry interpretation – were bound

---

[12]I.A. Richards, *Practical Criticism* (New York: Harvest Books, 1956), 11.

[13]Peters, *Speaking Into The Air*, 12.

[14]Ibid., 83. Peters finds the root of this economic principle in John Locke's belief that the meaning of language functioned like a kind of currency standard that keeps the signifiers of language from becoming inflationary and meaningless.

[15]Ibid, 12.

up with the idea that if given the correct tools, the reader of the translation could come to the "right" interpretation.[16] Or as Richards writes
in his essay "Toward a Theory of Translating," when different readers
approach the poem correctly, "there might be little we would then differ
about." Gentzler argues that "[s]uch a premise allowed Richards to sketch
an encoder/decoder communication model similar to those used by communication theorists."[17] Crucially, Richards is able to posit that translation
is possible precisely due to the communication paradigm that so often rejects translation as a corrupting force: the idea that there is an authentic
kernel of poetry outside of the words, an interiority beyond the versioning
of the words. Cultural difference is something the translator can overcome
by translating the essence of the poem, an essence that exists outside of
the language. It's within the language itself - the words and literary devic-
es - that the poem becomes vulnerable to deformation if the reader is not
properly educated and discriminating enough.

We can see the results of that influence in the pedagogic and aesthetic mottos made famous by the Iowa Writers Workshop: "write what you know"
and "find your voice."[18] Behind the phrase "write what you know" is a
profoundly regionalist model urging writers not to stray into the strange
world beyond their home, not to subject themselves to "foreign influence."
More importantly perhaps, it also suggests a limit to fantasies and stylistic
excesses: don't explore things you don't know. The goal is to "find" one's
"voice" to communicate this interior essence. Writing is construed as a
voice – i.e. not-writing – moving poetry back to the Socratic ideal of speaking with peers. Another key component of this motto is that you "find"
your "voice": it is natural, it comes from within, it is not artifice and it is not
foreign. It is not surprising that Hayden Carruth excluded any translation
from his seminal, program-era anthology *The Voice That Is Great Within You*.
Most importantly, it's a voice because it imagines the reader-writer relationship as one between friends talking, friends "communicating," resisting
the transgressive circulation of modern society.

4.

It is remarkable how closely anxieties about communication failure map
onto anxieties about translation. As premiere translation theorist Lawrence Venuti has argued, in dominant US literary culture, translation is
dismissed as "a second-order representation... derivative, fake, potentially

---

[16]Edwin Gentzler, *Contemporary Translation Theories* (Bristol: Multilingual Matters, 2001), 16.

[17]Ibid., 16.

[18]For more about these mottos, see Mark McGurl's *The Program Era*.

a fake copy."[19] What is "lost in translation" is the illusion of "direct contact between interiorities." Drawing on Kittler, we might say the translation is a kind of "ghost" – flat and inhuman. It lacks interiority, authenticity. This might be why, as Daniel Tiffany demonstrates in *Radio Corpse*, the corpse is such an important metaphor in discourses about translation: Either the translation is already dead, or all foreign texts are corpses which must be revived, given an "afterlife" (as Walter Benjamin notes in his seminal essay "The Task of the Translator"). Peters argues that the rise of the communication ideal led to the proliferation of "spiritualist" practices: acts meant to provide direct access to the dead. There's a necrotic dimension to our anxieties about both communication and translation. This is because Western emphases on voice, interiority, and meaning repeat Western preferment of the 'spirit' over the 'body'. Translation is the persistence of the body, but it also enfigures the potential of the body to change, to rot or release emanations. Translation scandalizes the self-sameness of human presence; it is the corpse or the ghost that follows too late or too soon on human presence.

As with the discourses that idealize communication, there is an erotic dimension to the rhetoric of translation. In Socrates' erotic anxieties about the written word, we can sense the origins of the most pervasive metaphor for translation: the idea that a translation is either "faithful" or "free." For many critics, the degree of a translator's "fidelity" is the only way of even discussing the translation. Translation's proliferation of language ruins the monogamous illusion of the original. Peters almost makes this connection between communication and translation when he writes: "*The Phaedrus* is about messages lost in transit and illegitimate couples."[20] In *The Phaedrus*, the transgressive circulation of the written word creates an erotic power imbalance because the reader and writer may not know each other, may not be part of the same cultural context. When we apply this critique to the category of writing that is translation, these anxieties are intensified because not only may the writer be a stranger to the reader, the words themselves are not even the stranger's words. Reading works in translation is even more treacherous, more erotically troubling than just reading written words.

This imbalanced power dynamic puts the translator in an impossible situation: she cannot totally give up her autonomy to the foreign text but she also cannot assert her own autonomy, because that would tamper with the authenticity of the foreign text. The translator cannot be too slavish and at the same time cannot dismiss the original. It is notable that Robert Low-

---

[19] Lawrence Venuti. *The Translator's Invisibility* (New York: Routledge, 1995), 7.

[20] Peters, *Speaking Into The Air*, 51.

ell's self-consciously "unfaithful translations" were published with the title *Imitations*, suggesting the difficult position of the translator: either she is so "faithful" or "literal" that she erases her sense of agency entirely, becoming "slavish," or she is so "free" that her work becomes mere "imitation," which is to say, not "free" at all, but completely "derivative" (to invoke Venuti's phrase again). In other words, translation is impossible. As a result of this impossibility, a lot of suspicion is directed at the translator and her version of the text: Is this foreign text good enough to warrant being read in translation? Is the translation good enough? Am I being fooled by the translator's counterfeit copy? Is this translation a hoax? Is there even an original? These fears suggest that translation troubles the framework of the monoglossic illusion. The danger of translation is not just that it makes the original yet another version, but that it infects the entire literary culture with a proliferation of versions. The economy of taste breaks down.

5.

Communication theory, the workshop aesthetic and translation have a complicated, politically-charged relationship. Lawrence Venuti has drawn attention to the political dimension of this nexus, suggesting the ways that the "plain style" aesthetic so dominant in US writing programs has a strong tie to US hegemony. Venuti argues that in contemporary US literary discussions, the translator – and the translation process – has to be "invisible" in order to maintain the illusion that "the author freely expresses his thoughts and feelings in writing, which is thus viewed as an original and transparent self-representation, unmediated by transindividual determinants (linguistic, cultural, social)."[21] The erasure of the process of translation produces "the illusory effect of transparency that simultaneously masks its status as an illusion: the translated text seems "natural," i.e., not translated."[22] He points out that this "plain style" aesthetic tends to render translations – as well as the translation process – "invisible." Few translations are published, and translations tend to be valued to the extent that they sound like US "plain style" works. Venuti has effectively argued that the "plain style" of the program era has gone hand in hand with the worldwide hegemony of US culture and the English language: this geopolitical power construct renders foreign literatures and cultures "invisible", the US central. The regime of "plain style" aesthetics participates in a US hegemony – established primarily through military, political, economic and legal actions – by denying the cultural specificity of the rest of the world. The ideal of "communication" turns cultural specificity into an obstacle to be overcome. The relationship between communication theory, translation

[21]Lawrence Venuti. *The Translator's Invisibility* (New York: Routledge, 1995), 6.

[22]Lawrence Venuti. *The Translator's Invisibility* (New York: Routledge, 1995), 15.

and US hegemony is even more complex than Venuti's analysis. As Eric Bennett has shown in his book *Workshops of Empire*, the influential Iowa Writers Workshop, which was founded by communication theorist Wilbur Schramm, grew into prominence in large part as a response to Cold War anxieties. Paul Engle, who took over from his mentor Schramm, fund-raised to a great extent on the idea that the Writers Workshop provided a model of US cultural greatness with literature that was middle-of the-road aesthetically as well as apolitical. A key component of Engle's sales pitch for grants and sponsorships was that the Writers Workshop would show the rest of the world that America was creating the best literature. Building on Bennett's work, Richard Jean So has focused on the way this aesthetic was used as propaganda in Asia, where the US was combatting the spread of communism. As So points out, the International Writers Program (Engle's later off-shoot from the Writers Workshop) aimed to bring foreign writers into Iowa to learn how to write according to the Iowa aesthetics, who then would return to their homelands "spread[ing] the gospel of democracy and individual freedom."[23]

The IWP had a specific interest in using the Iowa aesthetic to teach writers from "developing nations" to feel "empathy." So explains:

> … foreign students at Iowa had to be taught empathy—a social scientific buzzword that Engle took from his friend and colleague Wilbur Schramm, a proponent of modernization theory and a founder of communication studies in the US. Learning activities at the IWP, informal as they were, focused on inculcating students with an empathetic disposition. The hope was that such students would embrace this disposition in their writing and that the literature they produced at Iowa and beyond would manifest this quality. For Engle, this pedagogy constituted the backbone of the broader plan of modernizing Asia. Many of the students in the 1960s and 1970s came from Taiwan, South Korea, and Japan—all postwar Asian developing nations. Thus, the invention of the IWP is also a story about socialization and pedagogy, and how this pedagogy came to take on global implications.[24]

The workshop aesthetic, which came out of communication theory, was used to convince foreign writers to believe in a key component of communication theory: the model of interiority accessed through "empathy." We can see in this treatment of foreign students not just how the "plain style" aesthetic was spread to the rest of the world, but also how this aesthetics

[23]Richard Jean So. "The Invention of the Global MFA." *American Literary History*, 2017, Vol. 29(3), 500.
[24]"Global MFA," 501.

was based on a "communication"-based model, as well as how this communication paradigm – however pleasant it may seem in abstraction – can be deployed not just as a cultural hegemony but also political imperialism.

6.

The pervasive rhetoric of protecting this idealized communication from the sensationalistic, excessive and foreign participates in what George Bataille called a "restrictive economy." According to Bataille, this rhetoric – capitalist, Protestant – uses the logic of "utility" to create a culture in which "pleasure" is restricted to "a moderate form," while "violent pleasure is seen as *pathological*."[25] Against the "restricted economy," Bataille posits poetry not as something that needs protection against excess but as "synonymous with expenditure," part of the "so-called unproductive expenditures: luxury, mourning, war, cults, the construction of sumptuary monuments, games, spectacles, arts, perverse sexual activity…"[26] In Bataille's view, poetry is not what must be protected against loss; it is the waste, the loss. If poetry "communicates" it does not communicate economically but inflationarily. In Richards' description of the threat of "mania" and "orgy" and "inaccessibility" we can see the communication ideal as well as its other: the Bataillean "general economy" and the squandersome "expenditure" of poetry. Poetry is loss. Poetry spends and spends. Poetry is the "orgy of verbomania." Poetry is the excess that the "restrictive economy" of ideal communication must protect itself against. If poetry is in the "loss," and translation precipitates poetry's loss, then translation and poetry are not opposites. Instead, they co-constitute each other.

It was this co-volatility of poetry and translation that Joyelle McSweeney and I wanted to foreground in *The Deformation Zone*. The model of the deformation zone rejects the communication ideal by positing that poetry – and its translation – are in "transgressive circulation," pulling readers and writers into an unsettled and unsettling flux. As Socrates pointed out, transgressive circulation is in large part an issue of power: the foreign text's power over our bodies. As such, a number of other power-issues are involved: US literature's emphasis on agency and interiority necessarily needs to control the influence of the foreign. One aspect of this anxiety is the dominant communication-based ideal in which the reader of a poem remains in control: the reader "accesses" the meaning of the poem. But as Steven Shaviro – drawing on the work of Leo Bersani as well as Gilles Deleuze – argues in his book about film, *The Cinematic Body*, the pleasure of art can be "masochistic": "The self is repeatedly shattered by an ecstatic

---

[25]Georges Bataille, *Visions of Excess: Selected Writings 1927-1939*, Ed. Allan Stoekl (Minneapolis: University of Minnesota Press, 1985), 116.
[26]Ibid., 118.

excess of affect."[27] (The urge to restrain this dynamic is what I'm going to discuss as the fear of "foreign influence" in the next chapter of this book.)

Poetry transgresses boundaries – of personhood, of nationhood – so the illusion of interiority and communication must be maintained through constant pathologization and dismissal (such as the rhetoric of the impossibility – and even erotic immorality – of translation). In its transgression of boundaries, poetry – and particularly poetry in translation – punctures what Bakhtin described as the monoglossic illusion of a hierarchical, stable language, and of stable, unified texts. Bakhtin was right when he pointed out that--unlike in these monoglossic models,-- language is inherently heteroglossic, constantly opening to new usages and coinages, reshaped by dialects and ideolects. Where I differ from Bakhtin is the role of poetry in his model. Bakhtin held that poetry was necessarily monoglossic, shoring up national linguistic and cultural prerogatives. To me, it seems obvious that poetry can enact a zone of antic heteroglossia, and translation, dealing as it does in multiple languages, amplifies this energy. We might say that poetry is a heavily contested site, where some critics and poets attempt to maintain the monoglossic illusion of poetry, with its nationalist boundaries, even as others celebrate and participate in the noisy heteroglossia of poetry.

The deformation zone consists of texts in circulation. It is a site of utter changeability over and against the supposed fixed categories of 'domestic' and 'foreign', changing both the texts as they move and those authors and readers who receive and change and are changed by the texts.. The deformation zone is also inflationary. The deformation zone proliferates, generates copies of itself, invites versions, imitations. The key to the deformation zone is the volatility of the poem, the poem's ability to allure and overwhelm, the way it crosses boundaries, troubling ideas of originality and original context. In the deformation zone, both translator and reader are possessed by the foreign text, confirming all of Plato's anxieties about transgressive circulation. Yet this zone is not a cosmopolitan idyll that allows ideas and readers to cross boundaries effortlessly. Instead, the deformation zone acknowledges that translations deform: in acts of translation, there is violence done to the original, but there is also violence done to the target culture, to the translator. This violence, generated by the transgression of translation's circulation, is not something we should attempt to protect poetry from; instead we should recognize it as poetry's signature. We should accept and embrace it.

[27]Steven Shaviro, *The Cinematic Body* (Minneapolis: University of Minnesota Press, 1993), 56.

3

"AWASH IN MIMICRY": THE THREAT OF FOREIGN INFLUENCE

1.

In the Q and A session following a substantial and varied panel on the poetry of Paul Celan at the AWP conference in Minneapolis in 2015, the first
question asked by an audience member was "How can we make sure that
young American poets are not improperly influenced by Celan's poetry
without truly understanding it?" The panel responded by offering a variety
of possible solutions, such as reading the extensive secondary literature
about the poet or reading his letters and journal entries. For me, this seemingly innocent question points toward several issues involving translation
in US literary culture. Most importantly, it calls attention to the prevalent
suspicion of foreign influence, an influence which manages to traverse borders and contexts, destabilizing norms and hierarchies. The fact that it was
the first question of the session suggests that is has a great deal of urgency.
Why is the "improper influence" of a foreign author such an important
concern? And what might that tell us about the US literary culture?

In the scenario presented by the questioner, the anxiety is not over the
translator (two of Celan's English-language translators were on the panel, positioned as authorities), as is so often the case, but rather about the
receivers of these translations – the "young American poets." The innocent, ignorant enthusiasm for the foreign text makes a hoax out of the
translation, makes a counterfeit out of Celan. In their permeability, these
hypothetical young American poets become victims of kitsch, reverse al-
chemists who turn gold into trash by consuming the foreign literature in

translation and thus bringing this foreign influence into US poetry. These young poets occupy the site where the authentic poem is "lost," giving way to a dangerous counterfeit. They make American poetry vulnerable by failing to observe a hard border between US and international literature, and they make US poetry porous and unbounded, infirm, a body without firm borders. Such a hard border is entirely chimerical in the case of Celan: there can be no language border in the case of the refugee Celan, no 'expert reader' for a poet whose own writing makes a deformation zone of language, whose distended syntax demonstrates the fungible limit of language itself. Such an attempt to protect Celan from youthful zeal, and the youth from the seductive volt of Celan, is an attempt to control the limitless, lawless, volatile appeal of poetry itself, a volatility consummately embodied by Celan's own work. If Celan's work emits a signature, it is this irresistible fascination that is poetry's most indelible quality.

Adapting Mary Douglas's argument about "pollution symbolism"[28] – later used by Julia Kristeva in her writings about abjection – to poetry, we might say that the young poets are the sites of possible contamination. They risk confusing boundaries – between US and foreign poetry, between greatness and counterfeit – because they have not yet learned the important distinctions between what belongs and what doesn't. They do not yet know how to read poetry properly. Their shallowness – their lack of learning – may cause them to imitate bad models, or imitate good models for the "wrong reasons." (I imagine that the questioner at the Celan panel was concerned about Celan's use of neologisms, for example.) Because they have not been properly installed in the illusorily stable US tradition, they pose a threat to the tradition.

The threat of the foreign is portrayed time after time as a problem of false, improper, counterfeit or shallow "influence." This anxiety hides a greater concern: the fear that foreign literature will destabilize the native literature, flooding the culture with poems and ideas that are not properly installed in the reigning tradition. Perhaps even more fundamentally, these anxieties suggest a concern not just about the dangers of foreign influence, but of artistic influence itself: the "potentially deregulating power"[29] of encountering a work of art, of opening oneself up to a work of art, the act charged by the erotic, masochistic dimension of transgressive circulation. Both translation and the masochistic model of reading challenge the fundamental ideal of mastery.

[28]Mary Douglas, *Purity and Danger: An Analysis of the Concepts of Pollution and Taboo* (1966, reprint, London: Routledge, 2002).
[29]Hoogland, *A Violent Embrace*, 2.

2.

George Steiner portrayed the threat of foreign influence with great precision in *After Babel*, his canonical but controversial meditation on translation. I would like to read Steiner's text, in particular the essay "The Hermeneutic Motion," *against the grain* to re-envision the radical potential of translation in the threat of the foreign. In his book, Steiner portrays all communication acts as acts of translation. Like Peters' various communication theorists in *Speaking Into the Air*, Steiner realizes that translating one's interiority inevitably opens that interiority up to corruption and destabilization, the dangers of communication failure. Steiner does not appear to believe in an ideal communication that eludes "communication failure." There is no Athens-before-writing for him; we are "after Babel." Steiner describes all acts of communication as necessarily involving the violence of translation. This is particularly true of inter-cultural acts of translation. In order to find a "dynamic equilibrium" for translations, and to prevent the foreign influence from becoming disabling, Steiner breaks down the act of translation into a "hermeneutic motion" consisting of four parts: "trust," "aggression," "incorporation" and "restoration of balance," stressing the dangers of translation and the importance of incorporating the foreign into the domestic order. Without such proper "motion," Steiner fears translation can lead to a country being "awash in mimicry," disabled by a flood of imitations, counterfeits, kitsch.[30] Of course it is just this that interests me about translation. This is why, when read *against the grain*, Steiner's diagnosis of the supposed threat of translation reveals its political and aesthetic potential.

Steiner's essay stresses the pervasiveness of violence in translation. With his "hermeneutic motion," he seeks to negate this violence through a largely economic framework that stresses balance and harmony. The first step of Steiner's motion is "trust": the translator has to trust that the text he or she is about to translate is worth translating. This means that the text has to have some interior meaning which is worth extracting. Steiner notes that the initial trust is often "betrayed, trivially, by nonsense, by the discovery that 'there is nothing there' to elicit and translate."[31] In other words, the foreign text could seduce the translator into trying to translate it, but then turn out to be not worth the effort. Steiner argues that "nonsense" as well as "poésie concrète" and "glossolalia" "betrays" the value of translation because such usages of language do not have an interior meaning which

---

[30]George Steiner, *After Babel: Aspects of Language and Translation* (Oxford: Oxford U.P., 1975), 315

[31]Ibid., 312.

the reader can grasp (and then translate) - either because there is no meaning (as in nonsense) or because their use of language is fundamentally that
of a foreigner, someone who does not have mastery over the language
(glossolalia). At the heart of this argument is an appeal to the communication ideal: meaning is something interior which gives value to language.

Going back to the AWP question, we can see how the fear of an "improper Celan" could be construed as a "glossolalic" or "nonsensical" Celan:
Celan's radical breaking-down and reconstitution of German might make
his poetry hard to "trust." We might say that the untrustworthy, suspi-
cious writing modes oppose the communication ideal by engaging in a
more squandersome, Bataillean anti-economy of language. Steiner's fear
of such wasteful language is similar to I.A. Richards' fear of "the orgies of
verbomania." There is a lack of meaning to give value to the text, a lack
which in turn creates a surplus: an excess of language without significa-
tion. In *Speaking Into the Air*, Peters finds an important predecessor for the
modern communication ideal in John Locke's economics-based model of
meaning as a kind of currency that gives value to language. According to
Peters, Locke describes "signs" as "property" which must be made useful,
and that "[s]igns without support from ideas are 'sounds without significa-
tion.'"[32] Ideas provide a kind of currency, without which language becomes
susceptible to inflation, proliferation and meaninglessness – or exactly the
charges that are regularly invoked to portray translation as a threat.

However, Steiner does not believe the risk of translation is limited to the
target culture. Once the foreign text has proven itself worthy of trust and
the translator translates it, the danger of transgressive circulation turns
around: the act of translation becomes a risk to the source text. In order
to grasp the meaning of the foreign text, the translator has to go into a
"mode of attack." Steiner gives the act of comprehension a number of violent metaphors: translation involves capturing something and bringing it
home; breaking a "code"; even "dissecting" the foreign text. The translator
must "penetrate" the foreign culture in order to "extract" the meaning as
if it were gold in some colonial enterprise. The result could be "leaving the
shell smashed and vital layers stripped."[33] As in Locke, the interiority or
meaning of the text is what has value. Unlike so many apologists for translation, Steiner does not see communication and violence in opposition.
Translation is an inherently violent act. The source language - the shell
that holds the meaning within it - might be left shattered. Steiner acknowledges the danger that the translator may leave the original "smashed" and
worthless, that the translation may render the original worthless because

[32]Peters, *Speaking Into The Air*, 83.
[33]Steiner, *After Babel*, 314.

the new version is "more ordered, more aesthetically pleasing." While I obviously reject Steiner's culturally biased and evaluative rhetoric here, he rightly recognizes that different versions of a text do not merely exist neutrally on two sides of a border. Instead these versions perpetuate a volatile—sometimes radiant, sometimes violent—relationship.

In fact, this volatility fuels Steiner's anxiety, which he dresses in abelist and xenophobic rhetoric. Steiner warns against the results of a translation that is not properly installed in the new culture. He warns that translating might "potentially dislocate or relocate the whole of the native structure." Like sexual intercourse, the translation can lead to "infection": "No language, no traditional symbolic set or cultural ensemble imports without the risk of being transformed."[34] And this infection may ruin our sense of self by disabling the supposedly intact native culture: "we may be mastered and made lame by what we have imported."[35] Steiner makes obvious the fears that underlie a lot of the anti-translation rhetoric of our culture: we may lose ourselves, who we are – as a nation, as individuals. Translation may undo our illusion of mastery, challenging widely held beliefs about evaluation and tradition by offering alternative views of history and canonicity. For Steiner, it appears that translation accentuates what Hoogland calls the "potentially deregulating power" of art. This deregulating experience may indeed transform our culture—and it is here that I both agree and depart from Steiner. Where he sees threat, I see promise. For it is here that translation's—and art's— aesthetic and political potential truly lies.

Steiner tries to alleviate this danger by creating an economic framework for incorporating the foreign, translated text into Anglo-American literary culture. Not only must the translator beware of losing him or herself, but the greater culture has to incorporate the translation into its context and literary lineage in order to avoid "inflation." If this is not avoided, the literary culture might be "awash in mimicry." Steiner sets up an economic model for translation: "Fidelity," he argues, "is ethical, but also, in the full sense, economic."[36] The translator must create "a condition of significant exchange.... ideally, exchange without loss."[37] It seems the threat of translation is that it might produce an excess that would ruin the economy of meaning and taste. Foreign texts are not just threatening because they bring foreign ideas into the target culture; they may in fact ruin the entire system of literature through sheer excess. Translation may make too many

---

[34]Ibid., 315.

[35]Ibid., 315.

[36]Ibid., 318.

[37]Ibid., 319.

texts, so that we may not be able to tell the good from the bad, and thus we may not be able to sell it. Translation is a Bataillean engine. Translation, like poetry, creates waste.

This inflationary, anti-economic, potentially disabling vision of translation lines up with the AWP questioner's view of the "young American poets" who – numerous, nameless – proliferate and cheapen the Celan poems by assuming his influence in an improper way. They do not grasp the interiority of the text - they can't because it is foreign to them, they do not have the authority of experts – and as a result they open themselves up to the disabling and destabilizing influence of the translations of Celan's work. As in Socrates' erotic anxieties, the transgressive circulation penetrates them, undoes their autonomy. Using Steiner's language, we can say that they are made "lame" by Celan's influence. They do not have mastery over Celan, and as a result they threaten the entire "restricted economy" of US poetry. At the heart of this anxiety is the ideal of communication, a stable notion of context and the sense of foreign influence as a threat. Rather than "communicating" between "interiorities," translation puts us under the potentially debilitating influence of the foreign: a foreign force that overtakes us in a "violent embrace." I of course am on the side of the students. Through transgressive circulation, I call upon those that have been assigned the supposedly denigrating terms of disabled, unwell, weak, conquered and foreign, to join in an unstable zone and emit destabilizing counterforces on the supposedly native culture that would exclude, marginalize, limit or control them.

3.

In an era defined by what Lawrence Venuti has described as "the global drift toward American political and economic hegemony in the postwar period,"[38] it is important to question exactly the kind of "mastery" that encourages a continued xenophobia against foreign literatures. The hegemony of the English language and US culture, which has resulted from its economic and military power, has ensured that many people around the world read and watch and listen to US cultural products even as children. Around the world, people are "awash" with American culture. Why is it so important then for US critics to keep out foreign influence? Rather than keep out foreign influence, I would argue that we should open ourselves up to foreign influence. If we read Steiner's essay *against the grain*, it tells us in great detail that works in translation have a destabilizing potential that is important in this age of imperialism, invasions, hegemony and neo-co-

[38]Venuti, *The Translator's Invisibility*, 15.

lonialism. Furthermore, Steiner's essay suggests the connection between capitalism and "mastery," between "restricted economies" and literary gatekeeping, communication and conservative aesthetics. By opening the gates to translation we transform dominant culture's anxiety *about* the foreign into a tool of counterpressure that can be used against the regimes of control and exclusion on every level.

We may even see something of Bataille in Steiner's recognition that translation is a "dangerously incomplete" act, that there is a fundamental economic imbalance in translation. There is no perfect translation in the sense of a perfect replication of an original. But if this is an impossible ideal, I propose we look at this imbalance as a key to what translation does: it creates imbalances, it ruins illusions of completion and mastery, it reveals the violence of not just translations themselves but of all poems. Any poem can infect the reader (or writer), can pull them into deformation zones.

4.

In her 2011 lecture on "influence" at East Anglia University, Joyelle McSweeney argued:

> It seems to me that a discussion of literary influence would benefit from an effort to think outside these structures and strictures. I'm for thinking of influence in terms of the dead metaphors of flow, flux, fluidity, and fluctuation, saturation and suppuration, inherent in the term 'influence' itself, influence as total inundation with Art, inundation with a fluctuating, oscillating, unbearable, sublime, inconsistent and forceful fluid.[39]

There is in poetry (and art) the potential for "inundation," saturation. Poetry can overwhelm us. It can put us under its influence like a drug. McSweeney argues that this "flux" and "inundation" runs counter to the linear, hierarchical, patrilineal model of influence in the work of critics like Bloom and Vendler. Translation seems to foreground a danger that is present in all powerful poetry. Without the proper, canonical, patrilineal context of tradition, we are more vulnerable to art's potentially debilitating influence. Part of the reason US critics are threatened by translation and attempt to quarantine it is because it takes us out of the heavily disciplined sphere of American poetry, where scholars have established lineages and evaluative narratives to control such improper influence. Without the stabilizing effect of these national traditions, foreign artworks become

---

[39]Transcription was posted on Montevidayo: http://montevidayo.com/2011/06/influence-deformation-zone-a-telex-from-solaris/

dangerously volatile. The need to control the influence of foreign poetry comes out of the need to control poetry itself.

Poetry is not that which we extract or "access," but something that influences us, something that moves in transgressive circulation. The influence that US literary culture wants to contain is not the kind of influence that Bloom talks about: one poet is influenced but then makes the influence his own and emerges a strong, autonomous poet in control of poetry. No, this is that other influence, the one that is like the drug of art, the one from which we don't emerge whole, in charge, productive. The threat of poetry, like the threat of translation, is the threat of a foreign influence. The recipient of any artwork is in danger of being infected, or even of having the top of their head taken off, of being made part of the artwork. And when that happens, writers may indeed start channeling foreign writers, might lose their illusions of mastery: might find thems elves "awash in mimicry."

4

KITSCH, or THE HOAX OF TRANSLATION

1.

Just as modern poetry has pervasively defined itself against translation, much of modern art (including literature, but also the visual arts) has defined itself against some notion of "kitsch" – the inauthentic, the fake, the hoax, the overdone, the "too much." But it has been very hard for critics to put their finger on what exactly is kitsch. In his recent book *My Silver Planet*, Daniel Tiffany has made a fascinating and important discovery: the origin of the notion of a kitsch art – indulgent, counterfeit, sentimental, empty – can be found not necessarily in the growing mass production of the late 19th century, but in 18th century poetry discussions about the ballad revival, gothic hoaxes and – more generally – "poetic diction." Since then, kitsch seems to have become increasingly common and increasingly threatening ("It is said to be at once parasitic, mechanical, and pornographic," associated with homosexuality and moral decay[40]). Modernists like Clement Greenberg defined modern art in heroic opposition to kitsch. However, most of the time kitsch is more malignant than a mere stand-in for the unauthentic. Even as it is dismissed as passive and lacking, kitsch takes on a parasitical, dangerous character. The German writer Hermann Broch compares the relationship between true art and kitsch to that between "Christ" and "Anti-Christ," and argues that kitsch is "lodged like a foreign body in the overall system of art."[41] I'd like to pick up on this connection between kitsch and the dangerously foreign. And I would like to explore how this dynamic pertains to the way we discuss translated texts, those foreign bodies lodged in our system of literature.

Daniel Tiffany, *My Silver Planet: A Secret History of Poetry and Kitsch* (Baltimore: Johns Hopkins U.P., 2014), 1.

Hermann Broch, "Notes on the Problem of Kitsch," *Kitsch: The World of Bad Taste*, ed. Gillo Dorfles (New York: Bell Publishing Company, 1969), 68.

2.

One of Tiffany's most striking examples of kitsch rhetoric is the preface to the *Lyrical Ballads*, in which William Wordsworth rejects Thomas Gray and the gothic Graveyard poets for their "gaudy and inane phraseology." Tiffany points out that an important reason for Wordsworth's rejection of these poets is that their poetic diction is influenced by foreign works (Latin, Greek) in translation. Wordsworth argues that this causes them to write in a poetic way that interferes with his ideal of the poet as "a man speaking to men" in "the language really used by men." Anti-kitsch rhetoric is thus not just intertwined with poetic diction, but also with translation and foreign literature: foreign literature leads to the contamination of the language "really used by men." Perhaps the problem is that language influenced by translation is poetic, worthless, non-utilitarian – as in Bataille's "general economy" – because it is foreign, tainted, ineffective. In other words, it is not "used by men" - instead it "uses" men, infecting them and compromising their autonomy. There is something not just fake in the "gaudy" language influenced by the foreign, but perhaps there's also something deceptive, evil, much like the gothic hoaxes Tiffany describes elsewhere in the book.

In American literary discussions, critics are still using Wordsworth's model of rejecting the poetic or flowery as somehow deceitful. Over the past few years, there has been a steady stream of such essays – usually published in publications like *Writer's Chronicle* (the official journal of the Associated Writing Programs) and *Boston Review* – usually written by older poets, reprimanding the supposedly shallow younger poets. For example, Gregory Orr has written several essays attacking the flowery and poetic as somehow "elite," invoking Wordsworth explicitly as an icon of democraticness.[42] Similarly, Tony Hoagland has attacked the younger American poets for being "skittery" – why can't they just come out and say what they want to say? Because they are "under the influence," they have lost their own personhood to art's maleficent intoxication; they are "skittery" – lacking in strength and mastery.[43]

Not only do such articles invoke Wordsworth's argument that there is something inherently democratic and preferable about "man speaking to men," but they also invoke the implied rhetoric that there is a hoax about the "gaudy" – that these younger poets have been tricked or are trying to trick the rest of us. It's the job of this older, more prominent poet to set them straight. This rhetoric also ties into a lot of rhetoric that associates

[42]Gregory Orr, "Foundational Documents and the Nature of the Lyric," *The Writer's Chronicle* (Oct./Nov. 2014).

[43]Tony Hoagland, "Fear of Narrative and the Skittery Poem of Our Moment," *Poetry* (March 2006).

kitsch not only with tastelessness but also willful deceit. Or as Matei Căli-
nescu sums it up: "Kitsch may be conveniently defined as a specifically aesthetic form of lying."[44] The foreign body is lodged within our system, an
"Anti-Christ" fooling us into thinking it's a "Christ." Not only does kitsch
interfere with the communication paradigm, it actively undermines it. Not
only does it get in the way with its excess of "skittery" artifice, it pretends
to be something it is not. Kitsch is a hoax.

3.

The sense of kitsch as a hoax can be found perhaps most influentially in
the work of US (failed) poet and (successful) art critic Clement Greenberg.
In his massively influential essay "The Avant-Garde and Kitsch," Greenberg defines a heroic avant-garde as a rigorous, necessarily small group
fighting the forces of kitsch, which consists of mass-culture and – notably
bad poetry, poetry that is "too poetic". According to Greenberg, kitsch –
the result of the "decay" of society – has "far greater immediacy" than
"serious" art, and as a result, leads to a lazy readership: "In the end the
peasant will go back to kitsch when he feels like looking at pictures, for he
can enjoy kitsch without effort."[45] Jacques Rancière has traced this kind
of rejection of an art of "effects" back to the 19th century, when elitist
critics rejected the tasteless over-stimulation of mass culture.[46] Greenberg
argues that the avant-garde resists this over-stimulation of mass culture by
providing an authentic art that communicates rather than overpowers. In
this regard, his theory resembles the quite conservative New Critics and
their "communication" ideals. One of the key points for both the New
Critics and Greenberg is that authentic art demands practice. You have to
work for it; as a result, you become more sensitive. You don't need so much
stimulation. This is the opposite of Bataille's luxurious poetry: art as the
purest expression of bourgeois work ethic.

Although Greenberg does not discuss translation, the foreign has a strong
presence in his rhetoric. To begin with, discussions of the authentic against
"imitations" inherently tie into discussions in which translations are dismissed for being untrue. Further, such discussions privilege a select few
as authentic - while dismissing the masses as fake and tasteless. In his rejection of these masses as unsophisticated, Greenberg repeatedly invokes
the foreign. Perhaps most striking is the way he uses the "Russian peasant" as an exemplary consumer of kitsch. For some reason it is not just
the peasants who serve as the prototypical consumers of kitsch, but *foreign*
peasants. Most important is Greenberg's trouble maintaining a clear line

---

[44]Matei Calinescu, *Five Faces of Modernity* (Durham: Duke U.P., 1987), 229.

[45]Clement Greenberg, "The Avant-Garde and Kitsch," *Art and Culture* (Boston: Beacon Press, 1961), 18.

[46]Jacques Rancière, *The Future of the Image* (London: Verso, 2009).

separating the rigorous, muscular avant-garde from the decadent "Alex-andrism" of the exotic. Greenberg associates kitsch with "Alexandrism" – by which he means a kind of decadent, imitative aesthetic. But the word comes from the Egyptian city of Alexandria, and Greenberg is troubled by Yeats' obsession with Byzantine art because Byzantium is of course "very close to Alexandria." And not just in terms of geography: Yeats glorified Byzantium as an icon of art for art's sake. Greenberg wants to position the avant-garde against the decay of kitsch, but Yeats – for Greenberg a high modernist "avant-garde" poet – is obviously drawn to the exoticism of Byzantine art. Again we are drawn into the way kitsch is a trap, a hoax, a lie that by blurring "Christ" and "Anti-Christ" leaves us – to bring back Steiner – "awash with mimicry," unable to tell the authentic from the fake.

4.

In modern and contemporary US literary discussions, translation itself is treated with a kind of dubiousness that suggests fear of a hoax.[47] Transla-tors who work on foreign writers that are not already very canonical are constantly faced with questions about the authenticity of their projects: How do I know that this foreign author is good enough to be translated? How can I tell if your translation is faithful? How do I know that this poet isn't just someone you invented? When I first began to translate Aase Berg's work, several people asked me if I had not simply made her up. To be a translator is to assume to role of a hoaxer, someone who might be undermining the quality and trustworthiness of literature (and taste).

Further, Wordsworth's rejection of the "gaudy" language influenced by foreign works reminds me of American poetry's constant vigilance against "translatese." These are translations that sound foreign because the trans-lator – either intentionally or unintentionally – has deployed awkward syntax or odd word choices, thus foregrounding the foreignness of the translated text. Translation theorist Lawrence Venuti has argued that this tendency to dismiss foreign-sounding translations is part of a US imperi-alistic tendency to deny the "visibility" of the translator and the translat-edness of the text in order to promote the illusion of its own universality.

5.

The reason Wordsworth had to reject the Graveyard poets was that they were very popular. This is also, importantly, the case with a lot of trans-lated poetry. The reason so many taste-makers had to attack the "transla-

---

[47]And indeed there are still translation hoaxes, for example Kent Johnson's atrocity kitsch Yasusada hoax purporting to have been written by a Japanese survivor of the bombing of Hiroshima.

tese" of poetry in translation is that it has proven highly seductive. Poets read in translation – poets like Rumi, Pablo Neruda and Vasko Popa, and more recently Tomaž Šalamun (perhaps the father of much of that much maligned "soft surrealism") and Kim Hyesoon – have proven very popular with American poets and readers. In response, critics often try to denigrate poets who are too much under the influence of foreign poets and movements. For example, "soft surrealists" is a common insult of American poets who are influenced by foreign Surrealists, but who are supposedly "light", ie. lightweight, because they are writing in the US, away from the politically urgent contexts in which these foreign Surrealists wrote. Critical anxiety over and denigration of such "soft surrealists" parallels the anxiety over inflationary poetry that circulates without the gold standard of meaning to secure its valuation. Not only is this critique reactionary, it neglects the acute domestic political crises that have typified America since before its inception as a nation—its foundation on slavery and genocide, and the perpetuation of racism, oppression, economic exploitation, and forever wars that lumber on in its domestic and foreign policy. In 2009 Stephanie Burt could float terms like "soft-surrealist cotton candy" to refer to such poets when she quotes fellow poet Jon Woodward:

> I usually duck out of a book before I read ten poems, especially if it's just soft-surrealist cotton candy... I had a helpful conversation with a friend the other day about contemporary poetry and all its entrenchments and trivialities. My friend has been reading ancient Athenian poets whose work is known today only in fragments, much of it lost forever. The implications of that really restored a sense of perspective for me.

This quote, which figures into Burt's essay, "The New Thing," exhibits many of the rhetorical tendencies I have discussed in this book, including the Socratic prizing of that ultimate native poet, the Athenian.. "Cotton-candy" connotes non-nutritiousness, superficiality, insubstantiality, and, yes, youth and its errors. These elements of anti-kitsch rhetoric implicitly set the cotton-candy poets against serious poets, who do the rigorous work of writing hard poetry. Or better yet, it suggests that the only true poets are lost poets from millennia ago. Elsewhere in the article, Burt – referencing Tony Hoagland – suggests that all these young poets are mere imitators, writing: "Almost all literary movements and moments expire in a crowd of imitators." These young, candy-addicted poets weakly imitating Surrealism are akin to the young poets improperly influenced by Celan at the AWP panel: The threat of the foreign is that it will actually seduce

Americans, especially young poets, and thus ruin their taste, rendering everything kitsch.

6.

While I advocate for rejecting such anxiety and opening up our boundaries to foreign influence, it is also important not to "domesticate" the foreign, to make it comply with US poetics. Lawrence Venuti has correctly advanced a critique of what he sees as the dominant method of "domesticating" translations, i.e. making the foreign texts seem as fluent and graceful as possible, and thus seeking to eliminate aesthetic differences that would challenge dominant US aesthetics. Against this practice, Venuti proposes a "foreignizing" translation that foregrounds its own translatedness. He wants the translator to signal to the Anglo-American reader that the text is translated, and thus to teach the reader about the limits of Anglo-American culture.

However, while I agree with Venuti's diagnosis of the hegemonic 'domesticating' bias in too many translations, I think that the deliberately 'foreignized' translation unexpectedly runs the risk of similarly maintaining a border rather than allowing it to break down and generate dynamic uncertainty. Further, the foreign text should not be instrumentalized as a pedagogical tool for US readers. The foreign text does not need to be made more foreign by the translator – the foreign text is already foreign. Perhaps more troubling, Venuti's models of foreignizing translation and its pedagogical goals are strikingly familiar – echoing US Language poets' call for disrupting syntax in order to generate a critical distance. In a sense, then, Venuti's seemingly revolutionary call for the 'foreignizing' translation complies with one of the dominant streams of US *domestic* poetics in the past fifty years. Thus, Venuti's foreignizing project inadvertently becomes a strategy for domestication.

What about the translation which is harder to identify as translated or native? What if US poets started to treat foreign texts not as something that needs to be "foreignized" but as a hoax we cannot uncover? What will that uncertainty do to the way we read American poets? Such a contamination of our critical faculties would perhaps threaten most of the hierarchical evaluative systems in place in our culture. In the essay I mentioned above, Hermann Broch writes that "the enemy from within... is more dangerous than these attacks from outside" because it's impossible to tell the difference between "Christ" and "Anti-Christ."[48]

[48]Broch, "Notes on the Problem of Kitsch," 62.

7.

In *Ecology Without Nature*, Timothy Morton identifies distance with aesthetics and immersion with "kitsch." Distance allows us to see ourselves as "beautiful souls," separate from all the abject horror of the natural world. In difference to the mastery of distance, Morton writes, "Kitsch exerts a fascinating, idiotic pull... Kitsch is the nearest thing in modern culture to the shamanic ritual object. Kitsch is immersive. It is a labor of love: you have to "get into it."[49] But, Morton importantly notes, kitsch is really "a sense of 'sheer stuff,' of sprouting enjoyment—the sinthome."[50] (Using Lacan, Morton defines the "sinthome" as "the materially embodied, meaningless, and inconsistent kernel of 'idiotic enjoyment' that sustains an otherwise discursive ideological field."[51]). Kitsch is sinthome, the stuff of art –unredeemed by the "gold standard" of conceptuality or interior meaning, to return to Durham Peters. Or as Morton puts it, "the aesthetic itself is, in this view, just a disavowal of kitsch that is, uncannily, its inner essence."[52] Any work of art – no matter how lofty – becomes kitsch if you are immersed in its idiotic pull: "All art becomes (someone else's) kitsch."[53] Art – poetry most of all – is at its heart always potentially kitsch.

Morton's solution to this impasse is not to attempt to "get out by the roof (high critique such as historicism)" because it distances us, allows us to retain our beautiful soul illusion. It is important not create a conceptuality that will redeem the "stuff": "Could kitsch, with its affective glow, also have a non-conceptual aspect that is even more radical?"[54] It's this radical non-conceptuality that Morton is after, because it's exactly in the "distance" of conceptuality that ideology "resides."[55] Instead, Morton advocates "delving into, even identifying with, kitsch, the disgusting-fascinating sinthome" abjected from "high, cool, critical art theory and theory-art."[56] By immersing ourselves in the kitsch, we can cause the culture to "vomit forth a sinthome."[57]

It may be useful to think about translation as a kind of sinthome for modern poetry: the counterfeit that must be posited in order for the authentic poem to exist. I am arguing that we should not try to avoid the kitsch-label

[49]Timothy Morton, *Ecology Without Nature* (Cambridge: Harvard U.P., 2007), 152.

[50]Ibid., 151.

[51]Ibid., 67.

[52]Ibid., 154.

[53]Ibid., 154.

[54]Ibid., 157.

[55]Ibid., 67.

[56]Ibid., 155.

[57]Ibid., 67.

on translation. By embracing the kitsch of translation — rather than trying to conceptualize it as a critique — we will not only keep ourselves from feeling like "beautiful souls" who translate as part of a flawed but ethical practice, but also perhaps attack the kind of conceptual distance that upholds taste, a taste that tries to rid art of its own "stuff," the kitsch that is at the heart of art itself. So if the sinthome of translation's impossibility is the flood and the infection, we should immerse ourselves in its flood, letting it infect us, letting it influence us.

Perhaps more importantly, translation may be a sinthome for the idea of poetry as high art. Translation — with its versions, its floods, its too-much-ness, its border-crossing infections — has to be denounced in order for a pure idea of poetry to exist. That is why Frost's famous quip is so seminal: translation exists in order to prop up an idea of poetry as the authentic. By insisting on reading translations — not perfect translations, not flawed translations, not translation as communication — as immersive and affective, by insisting on its impossibility and its simultaneous possibility, we can reject a pristine, high-art ideal of poetry.

7.

Discussions about translation are overwhelmingly defined by a sense of impossibility, a sense of inevitable failure. Everybody knows that not only is poetry "lost in translation" but also that translation is "impossible." Translations fail to be poems, instead becoming counterfeit versions. And it's perhaps here that my own thoughts about translation tie in with Tiffany's thoughts about "cheap signaling": translations are nearly always "aesthetic failures," seen as dangerous counterfeits in the eyes of literature's establishment. Translations are "knock-offs," imitations of the true English-language poems and akin to "verbal relics." Instead of upholding rules of taste, translation — at least at its most intensive — asks us to read for "discounted, vulgar, imitation," or "cheap signals."

5

BAROQUE ACTS OF CANNIBALISM

1.

In the spring of 2014, Stephanie Burt published an essay on a group of contemporary American poets which she described as "Nearly Baroque." In distinction to her codification of the "New Thing" a few years earlier, these "nearly baroque" poets seek, in poetry, "the opposite of simplicity, preferring the elaborate, the contrived." Burt defined these poets in terms almost entirely against her own tastes:

> But it can seem just simple enough in its goals. The twenty-first-century poets of the nearly Baroque want art that puts excess, invention, and ornament first. It is art that cannot be reduced to its own explanation, that shows off its material textures, its artificiality, its descent from prior art, its location in history. These poets want an art that can always give, or could always show, more.[58]

In essence, these poets are *almost tasteless*. In distinction to all the fears of "too much," these poets wanted to go too far in their exploration of artifice. Many people (including myself) have taken issue with the essay. For at least a decade prior to this essay, Burt championed decorum in poetry; the title of her 2009 volume of criticism, *Close Calls with Nonsense*, indicates the border between order and disorder, compliance and non-compliance, which Burt has sought to maintain. In this essay, Burt continues her project, appropriating a rhetoric of excess from various poetics – US and foreign – that she has previously proscribed and using this appropriated rhetoric highlight poets who *do not* challenge her sense of taste. In doing so,

---

[58]Stephen Burt, "Nearly Baroque," *Boston Review* (11 April 2014), http://bostonreview.net/poetry/stephen-burt-nearly-baroque.

she has written an essay not about "excess" but about poets who allow her to thematize excess, while protecting herself from the destabilizing force of excess. She wants the poets to be *nearly* baroque, not baroque. *Nearly* tasteless, not fully tasteless. What does it mean to be "nearly" tasteless? Is it just a way for Burt to appropriate poetic discussions that challenge her own takes on poetry? Does its "nearliness" suggest a stance of moderation and restraint that defends the poets (and Burt) against precisely the excessive impact of the baroque? What is the importance of that word, "nearly"?

2.

As Joyelle McSweeney has pointed out, Burt's essay almost completely ignores the use of the term "Neo-Baroque" in Latin American literature. McSweeney described the article as a "missed opportunity and a false erecting of a boundary."[59] Lucas de Lima took a harsher tone:

> After mulling over Joyelle's questions, I went all the way, adding to them. Why does Burt bother with the baroque in the first place? Instead of meeting the baroque halfway, why not come up with a more tailored concept (a la the Montevidayans) like the Gurlesque, the Necropastoral, or Atrocity Kitsch? Or even Burt's own "elliptical poetry" or "the New Thing"? Then it occurred to me just how important lack in the "Nearly Baroque" may be. I think the 'nearly' of [her] taxonomy troubles it in ways that Burt doesn't actually intend. In its admission to not quite living up to Severo Sarduy or Sor Juana Inés de la Cruz, the "Nearly Baroque" reads like the ultimate symptom of American literary provincialism. A provincialism the term itself takes to its limit, nervously marking it. As if the boundaries that prop up jingoist navel-gazing had to finally dissolve.[60]

For de Lima, Burt's article amounts to the same anxiety as the "too much" rhetoric: the loss of "canon control." Since "canon control" means the control of taste, this discussion is important to my own argument: the foreign "pollution" is a threat of undoing the kind of "control" that taste exerts over the national poetry. In addition, I want to invoke some of the writing on the "Neo-Baroque" coming out of Latin America, inviting it to devour nationalistic ideals of US poetry.

---

[59]Joyelle McSweeney, "I Want To Go All The Way," *Harriet Blog* (16 April 2014), https://www.poetryfoundation.org/harriet/2014/04/i-want-to-go-all-the-way.

[60]Lucas de Lima, "Provincialism at its Limits: On Stephen Burt's Very US-American 'Nearly Baroque,'" *Montevidayo* (18 April 2014), http://montevidayo.com/2014/04/provincialism-at-its-limits-on-stephen-burts-very-american-nearly-baroque/.

3.

Perhaps the most foundational Latin America writer of the Neo-Baroque
is Severo Sarduy. His essay "The Baroque and Neo-Baroque" explicitly
connects the term to a tasteless excess of artifice:

> From birth, the Baroque was destined for ambiguity, for semantic
> diffusion. It was the thick, irregular pearl - in Spanish barruco,
> berrueco, in Portugese barrocco - the rocky, the knotted, the
> agglutinated, density of the stone - barrueco, berrucco, or perhaps
> the excrescence, the cyst, something that proliferates, at once free
> and lithic, tumorous, warty; perhaps the name of the hypersen-
> sitive, even mannered pupil of the Carraccis – Le Baroche or
> Barocci (1528-1612); perhaps – fantastic philology – an ancient
> mnemonic device of Scholasticism, a syllogism – Baroco] Finally,
> in the denotative catalogue of dictionaries, those heaps of codified
> banality, the Baroque is defined as "shocking bizarreness" (Littré)
> or as "outlandishness, extravagance and bad taste."[61]

Sarduy's own critical prose - and Christopher Winks' translation of it –
follows the aesthetics of the "thick, irregular pearl" of the baroque: his
"thick" writing winds, enfolds, "proliferates." The baroque is both the
seemingly elevated and free, and the tumorous and warty. The key here is
that artifice is not the opposite of the bodily and "warty," as it is so often
viewed. It is not the abject, but something that collapses such distinctions.
Unlike so many contemporary US critics, Sarduy does not abject the bodily, the sickly, the too-much; he finds his art exactly in that space of "bad
taste."

In the words of Peters, we can say that Sarduy finds the poetic exactly in
the way language "proliferates," in "extravagance." For I.A. Richards (and
one might add, Burt, who follows in his New Critical lineage), it is important to learn how to do close readings of poems in order to properly access
the interior meaning of the text, and thus avoid any of the destabilizing
excess of what Richards calls "the orgy of verbomania." Diametrically
opposed to this stance, Sarduy reads precisely for the "tumorous" textures
of literature, the destabilizing excess. Sarduy's rejection of a restricted economics of expression is enacted in the many commas of this passage: the
piling up of similar words that seem to mutate ("barruco," "berrueco,"
"barrocco"). It is noteworthy that the poetic matter plays the same role for
both Richards and Sarduy: for both of them, the poetic is this texture –

---

[61]Severo Sarduy, "The Baroque and Neo-Baroque," Baroque New Worlds, Ed. Louis Parkinson Zamora and Monika Kaup (Durham:
Duke U.P., 2010), 270.

the "skin" - of the poem. The difference is that Richards wants to ensure that readers move through the skin, to the interiority, which provides a "currency" that redeems the poetic language despite its lack of utility. For Sarduy, the poetry is found precisely in this mutating skin. For Sarduy, artifice comes out of the skin's extravagant movement, an extravagance that Sarduy - and Wicks – enact in the "agglutinated" writing, with its long and unwieldy sentences. In Sarduy's description, the neo-baroque is a kind of "verbomania" that enacts the saturation of the reader, overwhelming the reader's borders and boundaries.

According to Peters, this verbomania is viewed as much an illness of the body as it is an illness of the mind. In *Speaking Into the Air*, he posits St. Augustine's duality between body and soul – in which the body necessarily corrupts the soul – as an important predecessor to the modern communication ideal. For Peters, the idea that language corrupts pure interiority follows the Christian model where the body corrupts the spirit. In Sarduy's writing on the baroque, language becomes bodily; it is like a "cyst" - but it is also a site of artifice - with great extravagant sentences. In a sense, Sarduy undoes not just the divide between spirit and body, communication and failure, but also between artifice and nature. For Sarduy, these binaries are abandoned in the "shocking bizarreness" of the neo-baroque.

4.

The connection between translation and the bad taste of the baroque is further explored in the equally important essay "The Rule of Anthropophagy" by Brazilian poet Haroldo de Campos. De Campos (in Maria Tai Wolff's translation) argues that the Latin American baroque is at its root involved in the process of translation, or "critical devoration… from the point of view of the 'bad savage,' devourer of whites – the cannibal." In contrast to the role of the "noble savage," performing the role of the "bad savage" does not involve "submission (an indoctrination) but a transculturation, or better, a "transvalorization."[62] The result of this "cannibalism" is an attack on "ontological nationalism," the kind that is asserted in all the essays that create the idea of a "national literature": "A new idea of tradition (anti-tradition) to operate as a counter-revolution, as a countercurrent opposed to the glorious, prestigious canon."[63] For de Campos, the mutating skin of the baroque poem not only offends the good taste of the "communication"-based model of poetry; it offers a counter-colonial aesthetic. It does not communicate, it "eats" – and there is a politics both in the idea

---

[62]Haroldo De Campos, "Rule of the Anthropophagy," Baroque New Worlds, Ed. Louis Parkinson Zamora and Monika Kaup (Durham: Duke U.P., 2010), 321

[63]Ibid., 323.

that it eats the colonial forces, and that it eats rather than communicates. The poem enacts a kind of violence but also a transformation.

What might translation have to do with this "carnivalized," boundary-devouring, postcolonial baroque? Part of the answer can be found in Frost's "lost in translation" definition of poetry and in the oft-repeated truism that translation is "impossible." In his essay "Impossible Effigies," Daniel Tiffany notes that

> ... the impossible, as Georges Bataille observes, overwhelms utility, truth, and meaning, and thus engenders through translation unspeakable (and inconceivable) forms of exchange. Indeed, the impossibility lodged within translation is itself death, madness – and originality.[64]

Rather than the perfected "well-wrought urn," translation becomes an effigy that puts in motion a strange economy; instead of a "restricted economy," it generates a "general economy." In this strange economy, we may not only interact with the alien world by absorbing or rejecting, appropriating or conquering, but instead by becoming alien to ourselves, losing our own sense of mastery – over the poem, over ourselves – and opening up new realms of sensory-overwhelming "verbomania." Instead of going through the text to find a communication ideal in its interiority, we have to devour the text carnivalesquely.

We can see the connection between the "madness" of translation and the baroque in Walter Benjamin's canonical and evocative essay "The Task of the Translator":

> While content and language form a certain unity in the original, like a fruit and its skin, the language of the translation envelops its content like a royal robe with ample folds. For it signifies a more exalted language than its own and thus remains unsuited to its content, overpowering and alien. This disjunction prevents translation and at the same time makes it superfluous.[65]

Here the original text – the fruit – becomes baroque, fashion, full of "folds." We might think about the baroque fold in the terms explored by Gilles Deleuze, as a way of undoing or troubling the simple binary between interiority and exteriority: there are folds, not interiors and exteriors. Similar to the way Deleuze's folds question the relationship between

[64]Tiffany, Radio Corpse,187.

[65]Walter Benjamin, "The Task of the Translator," The Translation Studies Reader, ed. Lawrence Venuti (New York: Routledge, 2012), 79.

interiority and exteriority, the folds of Baroque translations trouble the clear-cut distinction between original and translation. Rather than merely producing flawed copies, translation is involved in something complex, interesting and anarchic.

In his essay on the baroque, de Campos tries to capture this "convulsion" of language with his neologistic, "knotted" text:

> The "rogue tradition" would be another name for "carnivaliza-tion"; it operates retroactively on the Baroque, on the Baroque seen by Severo Sarduy as a Bakhtinian phenomenon par excellence: the ludibrious space of polyphony and of language in convulsion.

For de Campos, the folds of the baroque are "Bakhtinian." For Bakhtin, language is always in a state of heteroglossic flux, but leading institutions try to maintain the illusion of monoglossia, the sense of a "unite[d] and centralize[d] verbal-ideological thought, creating within a heteroglot national language the firm, stable linguistic nucleus of an officially recognized literary language."[66] This is a project with obvious political dimensions: the goal of monoglossia is "centralizing and unifying the European languages." Languages are, in other words, part of the building of the nation-state. Against this centripetal movement, there's a heteroglossic, centrifugal movement that is constantly corrupting the illusion of a pristine, true language. Bakhtin finds this heteroglossic force particularly evident "on stages of local fairs" where "the heteroglossia of the clown bounded forth, ridiculing all 'languages' and dialects." At this carnivalesque site (further explored in Bakhtin's book *Rabelais and His World*), "there was no language-center at all" and "all 'languages' were masks" because "no language could claim to be an authentic, incontestable face."[67]

Translation is constantly threatening to create a similar space where all languages become "masks" and the clown ridicules "all languages." The heteroglossic and the bad taste of clownery together form a de-hierarchizing force in Bakhtin's model, a force that de Campos finds in the baroque. But this is a baroque that can never be "nearly," it must always be "too much," must go all the way because it's exactly in its fully bad, tasteless clownery that it opposes the centripetal forces of official literary culture, and the nation state that culture defends.

---

[66]Bakhtin, The Dialogic Imagination, 271.

[67]Ibid., 271.

5.

If in Burt's discussion of contemporary US poetry, the baroque stands for the *nearly tasteless*, it stands to reason that the foreign is directly involved in issues of taste and kitsch. If kitsch is "a foreign body lodged in the overall system of art," there is an intimate relationship between the foreign and the bad, the translated and the tasteless. As I wrote in the first paragraph of this book, when translations are dismissed, they are dismissed in the terms similar to bad poetry: they are not just bad, they are counterfeit. And the counterfeit is dangerous because it challenges notions of the authentic and the fake—as well as the original and the copy, the inside and the outside.

Anti-kitsch rhetoric is, as I have argued, a defense against the foreign and an immersive aesthetics, an aesthetic that revels in the weird, the strange, the night, the poetic, the possibly inhuman element of art. Kitsch is a threat that has to be abjected because it is a site where boundaries are traversed: the "foreign body" of kitsch is "lodged" inside the system of tasteful, modernist art. It may be foreign but it is inside the system, traversing the boundaries between inside and outside, creating folds in the system. The "foreign body" of kitsch provokes anxieties because it creates connections that traverse hygienic boundaries: between real and fake, between English and foreign. Greenberg portrays it as dangerous because it ruins the hygienic boundaries on which taste is based.

But "bad taste" can have a radical, political dimension. As recent discussions in biology have shown, there are more bacterial cells than human cells in the human body - more "foreign bodies" inside our human bodies than human bodies.[68] These findings have led Timothy Morton to postulate about "nonselves" that are enmeshed in our surroundings rather than separate from it. Joyelle McSweeney has posited a "necropastoral" of poetics, "a political-aesthetic zone in which the fact of mankind's depredations cannot be separated from an experience of "nature" which is poisoned, mutated, aberrant, spectacular, full of ill effects and affects." This necropastoral zone "does not subscribe to humanism but is interested in non-human modalities, like those of bugs, viruses, weeds and mold." The necropastoral devours boundaries - between self and not-self, dead and alive, nature and human – and creates something like the baroque of De Campos. We might say that translation is like recent ecological thinking in its troubling of humanist boundaries.

[68]Heidi Lynn Staples, "Songs of Our Nonselves," *Georgia Review* (Summer 2017), https://thegeorgiareview.com/summer-2017/songs-of-our-nonselves/.

[69]Joyelle McSweeney, "What is the Necropastoral?," *Harriet Blog* (29 April 2014), https://www.poetryfoundation.org/harriet/2014/04/what-is-the-necropastoral.

6.

This gothic ecological thinking may also give us a model for reading translation baroquely, cannibalistically, abjectly. In his study of gothic ecological thinking, *Ecology Without Nature*, Morton makes a point of how kitsch's
tacky, slimy quality turns it into a kind of abject:

> The Ancient Mariner and Frankenstein are gothic and tacky. The
> tacky is the anaesthetic (unaesthetic) property of kitsch: glistening,
> plasticized, inert, tactile, sticky – compelling our awareness of
> perception; too bright, too dull, too quiet, too loud, too smelly,
> not smelly enough – subverting aesthetic property. Coleridge
> respected the tacky; he appreciated the ethics of calling sugar the
> crystallized blood of slaves. So did Mary Shelley: her monster
> story undermines the myth of Romantic genius. Both stories are
> about excessively material stuff, art-matter as pure extension.[70]

It seems to me that Morton is wrong to call this "anaesthetic"; rather it
seems over-aesthetic, an artfulness that cannot be contained by good taste
– the defense of a restricted society, the restraint of consensus culture –
but instead overwhelms us, infiltrating every aspect of our lives. It is this
"art-matter" that draws me into art, that enchants me. It does not provide
a direct contact between interiorities, regularized by a stable "context" or
monoglossic idea of "original reader." But it is not the traditional abject,
as "sugar" suggests something that is appetizing, even if nutritionally void.

Morton shows how art's matter intervenes in our life in a way that is quite
different from the typical politics offered up by academic readings of the
politics of poetry:

> "Beyond its cuteness (a reified version of Kantian beauty), an
> element in kitsch ecological imagery maintains this abjection,
> a formless, abject element, Bataille's informe... The bourgeois
> subject would rule forever if fascination and horror always
> resulted in spitting out the disgusting object. Ecological art is
> duty bound to hold the slimy in view."[71]

Like Tiffany, Morton sees a connection between kitsch and the abject, artifice and the "informe." Like Sarduy, Morton sees a politics in the tasteless,
the tumorous layers of skin. The tasteless and "slimy" attacks the "bourgeois subject." While a typical academic reading of poetry tends to em-

[70]Morton, *Ecology Without Nature*, 158.
[71]Ibid., 159.

phasize the ability to spit out the "disgusting" – whether a poem is seen as "subverting" ideology, or the critic reads the poem as a symptom of ideology, which the critic is then able to "spit out" – Morton sees the politics of not spitting, of holding "the slimy in view." I would add that it's not just "ecological art" that should hold the "slimy in view;" it is the role of all art in a hygienic society whose devotion to functionalism runs counter to art's shitty matter. Art is extreme, and in a consensus culture, art that challenges the consensus hierarchies becomes "kitsch " - something to be spat out.

5.

If we return to Peters' discussion of "communication," we can see that the baroque is art without "currency" in the Lockean model of communication; Sarduy's baroque gives us meandering skin, rather than access to an interiority. It gives us proliferation – maybe even the "orgy of verbomania" that Richards so feared when he set out to teach poetry-readers the correct method of close-reading. Removed from the proper frameworks of reading, the poem becomes kitsch, informe, art's enchanting matter. As we saw earlier, in the discussion of George Steiner, this anxiety is at the heart of so much fear of translation: the translation will lack currency, will cause inflation, will damage us because it takes a foreign poem and brings it into our culture, where it lacks the proper framework, where it may turn into a dangerous foreign influence that will enchant "young American poets" who don't know better. There is a profound connection between art's matter – kitsch, enchanting, "slimy" – and the foreign.

In Bataille's writing, the "heterogenous" matter is that which deals with the "unconscious" and the abjection of the body – precisely that which normal society finds "impossible to assimilate." But this urge to expel is also central to what makes it heterogenous. For Bataille, the heterogenous matter – like the non-utilitarian luxury of poetry – is at odds with the "restricted economy" of the homogenous society: "Homogenous society is productive society, namely useful society."[72] Steiner's urge to regulate works in translation can be seen as the urge to cleanse translations of their "heterogenous matter," their proliferative skins.

What makes translated texts "bad," or troubling, or antithetical to poetry has close ties to what makes any poetry bad: a quality of too-much-ness that is inevitably construed as a lack. There's too much art, not enough interiority. Art's matter gets in the way of the human interiority. It is thus clear why de Campos sees translation as a key to the Neo-Baroque – not

[72]Bataille, *Visions of Excess*, 138.

the perfect translation, but the devouring translation, a translation that unbalances the account, the wasteful translation, the translation that has to be expelled, but which like Kristevan abjection keeps crossing boundaries in acts of transgressive circulation.

6

TRANSLATING FAT: AASE BERG'S FORSLA FETT

1.

If much of American poetry treats translation as pollution, infection, the potential "loss" of poetry, Swedish poet Aase Berg's 2001 book *Forsla fett* is a poetry of pollution and infection, a book that holds the "slimy" both in the sense of the bodily and the trashily poetic – "in view," as Timothy Morton puts it in his call for a gothic ecopoetics. Unlike the kind of poetry that idealizes "communication" as the "contact between interiorities," *Forsla fett* creates an affective "deformation zone" in which what one might assume was interior and exterior seem to move Mobius-like, corrupting each other. If Locke argued that the concept is a currency that redeems the language, Berg's poetry is hopelessly inflationary "stuff." It was written during the author's pregnancy and the birth of her first child, and in part this is the subject matter. But unlike narratives that posit the experience of giving birth as an awakening, a moment of authenticity revealed, Berg's book construes the pregnancy narrative as necessarily counterfeit, fake, translated, a corrupted kitsch version. Although the book is short and consists of short, tiny poems, the effect is similar to the one Severo Sarduy uses to define of the baroque: "the rocky, the knotted, the agglutinated, density of the stone." I might even say that this little but excessive book has the beauty of a "thick, irregular pearl."

2.

The very title of the book indicates a foregrounding of materiality and mediumicity. The work sets in motion a circulation of "fat" and folds, a deformation zone. I translated "forsla" – which other translators have translated as "carry" or "haul" – as "transfer" to bring the f-consonance into the title, emphasizing the sound of the title. The sonic play and puns of the book - the fattening up of language, its transfer without origin or destination- undoes the communication ideal and the Christian binary of body and spirit that is one of its formative influences. Instead of body and soul, interiority and exteriority, Berg's poetry "vibribrates" between interior and exterior. Like Baroque texts that devour-translate originals and boundaries, or "necropastoral" ecological poetry that troubles the boundary between human and non-human, Berg's book folds the spirit and the body into a Mobius strip where the inside is outside and the outside inside. "Forsla" suggests transferring, but it doesn't tell us where. It might be a command ("Transfer this fat!") or it might be a part of a larger sentence ("I want to transfer fat"). Unlike the Lockean thinking about communication – where meaning gives currency to language, redeeming the sounds – the foregrounding of the physical feeling of the f-sound in one's mouth is word without currency. An unredeemed proliferation of language, an inflation of sounds and letters. But it is precisely in that unredeemed physical transfer that it affects me.

Unlike the pervasive model of the poem as communication of interiority, which renders the whole project of translation suspect, Berg's poem is largely based on baroque translations that find poetry in devouring the "skin" of the texts rather than displaying a mastery of some kind of interiority or meaning. Berg takes the language in *Transfer Fat* from a wide range of sources - from Stanislav Lem's *Solaris*, from Kubrick's *2001: A Space Odyssey*, and perhaps more importantly from scientific articles – largely in English – about the notoriously theoretical science of string theory. Berg's book drags these theoretical science texts and science fiction narratives into a bodily and abject zone which makes fat – exterior, amorphous – out of its concepts and allegories. For example, in the poem "Hal tid" ("Hal Time"), Berg takes Kubrick's disembodied computer Hal and, through the Swedish pun on the word "hal" – slippery – gives the computer a bodyness. In the same poem, the suicidal character Harey, whose body is constantly disposed of in *Solaris*, makes strange sounds: "frosh" and "krasslar". In these onomatopoetic words, language becomes physical in its nonsense. Both bodies and non-somatic language become physical, if unsettling. The name itself - "Harey" – is through its recontextualization in a zone full of fairytale animals, such as hares, turned into an adjective; it is made "harey," full of the sinewy bodyness of hares. This hare-language has a profound, saturating effect, not through communicating an interiority, but by

involving the reader in its deformation zone of hares, whales and strings.
Its useless excess gives not interiority or souls to the characters, but rather
gives them "thick, irregular" bodies.

3.

While in the traditional communication paradigm translation leads to the
loss of interiority because the word is just a vessel for meaning, in Berg
the poetry comes out of bringing – transferring, hauling, carrying – the
theoretical words of string theory into the bodily, corrupting deformation
zone of *Transfer fat*:

Harpalt

Harelotsen strängad
lockar till sig motsatt ton
strängen vibribrerar
dimensioner som ska
kröka Instrumentet

Hörseln har en spänntid
rycker fortare än strängen slår
harpa föder unge
lotsar unge över fälten
av det änny oberedda

Here's my translation:

Hare Critter

The hare conductor stringed
attracts the opposite tone
the string vibribrates
dimensions that will
crook the Instrument

Hearing has a strungtime
twitches faster than the string strikes
harpy births child
pilot child across fields
of the as-of-yet unprepared

In this poem, the theoretical language of string theory is made "harey": the language – vibrating, material – opens up an affective, baroque zone of proliferating sensations and associations. The word "palt" in the title is difficult to translate because it both invokes a slang for little animal but also "paltor" or rags. As Daniel Sjölin has noted, this is the opposite of Language Poetry: instead of emptying the words of connotation, it amplifies the sense of connotation. Here the language of string theory (vibrations, conductors, tones, instruments) is brought into co-influence with a very physical language of animals and birth-imagery, so that the "strings" might not derive from string theory anymore, but from the birth process (they become "umbilical strings" in another poem).

The transferring of fat - of turning the "foreign" language of string theory into physically visceral poetry, and vice versa - signals a totally different attitude toward the foreign than the prevailing American concept of "loss." Berg does not have a "proper understanding" of the string theory when she lets herself be influenced by its textures and the associations, convulsions that occur when she brings it into her poems. The zone of Forsla Fett doesn't operate according to the monoglossic ideal of a purified communication, but rather the body and the soul comingle in the text. This is not a "deep" but intensive engagement with foreign words. The string doesn't "vibrate," it "vibribrerar" (or "vibribrates"): by adding a couple of extra letters, Berg makes the signifier vibrate. Part of the result of such minor usage of language is a physicalization of the language that aligns Berg's work with Deleuze and Guattari's prescription for a "minor literature":

> Since the language is arid, make it vibrate with a new intensity. Oppose a purely intensive usage of language to all symbolic or even significant or simply signifying usages of it. Arrive at a perfect and unformed expression, a materially intense expression.[73]

Just as Gregor Samsa's language becomes a kind of nonsensical buzzing, so Kafka's language becomes "materially intense." It is not "earned" by the Lockean concept that helped shape the "program era" aesthetics of US poetry. Rather, it is "fat," unhealthy and "vibribrating" in the kind of "orgy of verbomania" that Richards correctly feared. Berg's poetry is not the failure of communication, but it is also not a communication of an interior message. This a poetry that does not want to communicate a message, but a mutancy. Berg's corrupt and corrupting language is not a failure to communicate but is the poetry itself.

------

[73]Gilles Deleuze and Félix Guattari, *Kafka: Toward A Minor Literature*, trans. Dana Polan (Minneapolis: University of Minnesota Press, 1986), 19.

4.

This is poetry that treats the Swedish language not as whole, complete, masterable, but as a deformation zone through which foreign languages might enter, influence and "vibribrate." It is also a book in which the Swedish language itself becomes strange and strangely intensive. This aesthetic challenges the notion of "original context" on which so much of translation discussions hinge. Not only is it shot through with various "foreign languages," but the Swedish itself is foreign, anti-fluent, "harey." *Forsla fett* is a book that foregrounds the poem as a "deformation zone," an ambient space where the Swedish language goes through all kinds of permutations: words, connotations, meanings, letters are put into flux, circulation. For example, the word "val" can mean "whale," "election" or "choice" depending on the syntactical and narrative context, and Berg brings out this volatility innate to the word. In the ambience of the book – created by its broken syntax and puns – the word becomes multivalent.

If you look at the poem "Mamma val" you can see the complex way it deforms the Swedish language, exposing the Swedish language as foreign even to itself:

Mamma val

Amma val
Valyngelskal
Ge harmjölk,
alla val är
samma val

And in my translation;

Mom Choice

Nurse whale
Whalebroodshell
Give hare-milk
all whales are
the same whale

Does the title, "Mamma val," mean "Mamma whale" or "Mamma choice" (or "Mother Whale" to invoke *Mother Goose*)? The line "nurse whale" suggests that the "val" should be "whale"; but "all choices are the same choice" make perhaps more sense than "all whales are the same whale." The versions multiply within the text itself, even as one never gets the feeling that this could mean "anything." Its meaning is very specific, but it's a "vibribrating" meaning, "materially intense" and physical, not in contrast to a "meaning" but as part of the meaning.

To make matters even more complicated, there's also the neologism of "harmjölk," a compound word that could either consist of the verb "har" (to have) or the noun "hare" (hare): "give have-milk" or "give hare-milk"? The whole text is full of these neologisms, and often they invoke the repetends of the text (whales, hares, choices, nuts, blubber, fat). For example, in one poem we get the strange "valyngelskal" (whalebroodshell") and in another we get "fittstela rullbandsfettflod" ("cuntstiff loopstrackfatflood"). Rather than progressing narratively or rhetorically, the book moves by the devouring and termiting of the Swedish rules for combining words into new words; it moves by "raising fat."

This aberrant abuse of Swedish grammar betrays not the monoglossic ideal of mastery, where the language is "spirit made flesh." Rather, this is poetry that makes Swedish - and thus, in translation, English – language made strange. The strange effect of these odd neologisms is that they taught me as the translator to misread even standard compound words as neologisms. Thus when I got to the poem "Späckhuggaren," I read it not as the correct compound word for "killer whale" but for a neologism combining the words "späck" and "huggaren" – "The blubber biter."

Späckhuggaren–

här hänger hugget
väntande på späck
i många tusen år
av långsamhet

In translation:

Blubber Biter –

here hangs the bite
waiting for blubber
for many thousand years
of slowness

Through this breaking-down and recombining of words, Berg finds a materially intensive "blubber" language inside the standard Swedish words.

This logic can be seen in the following couplet from "Vattenskräck" ("Hy-
drophobia" or "Water Horror"):

Vi som däggdjur, äggdjur, valnötsdjur
föder ogärna levande ungar

These lines could be translated in a "correct" way like this:

We as mammals, egg animals, walnut animals
prefer not to give birth to live young

But the hyper-combinational atmosphere of the text has taught me not
to read these "fluently" but rather to read the compound words for their
parts. "Däggdjur" is the standard word for mammals, but Berg's book es-
tranges this word, making me see it for its two root words: "dägg" and
"djur" ("suckle animals"). To make matters even more complex, the text
has taught me to look for the word "val" ("whale") through the constant
repetition of the word, so that I see the "val" (whale) in "valnöt," the standard word for "walnut." So that there's some of the blubber of the whale
in the "walnut animal." I translated this as "whalenut animals" to invoke
this pun as much as possible. The poem – and my translation of the poem
– makes the standard word "walnut" if not "harey" then "waley," or maybe "birthy," saturating the language itself with the abject associations of
childbirth. The abject is not just written about, but brought into the very
dynamic of signifier-signified relationship, making "slimy" the puristic,
communication-based model of language.

When this kind of neologistic energy is combined with the puns of "val,"
the results are startling. For example, when in "Öppna väljaren" we come
to the word "oval", which is the standard word for "oval," but which contains the prefix "o" ("un") and "val." Thus, I translated it as "unwhale."
The neologistic, punning ambience denatures my reading of even the
most common words. For example, one poem is called "Vågar," the standard word for "dares." But the poem contains oceanic imagery, causing me
to find in the title also the word "vågor" – "waves." So that I translated the
title as "Darewaves." Similarly, after repeated usages of the word "hare" I
can't help but read the "hare" in the standard word for "harpoon," which
in my anti-fluent reading that becomes "harepoon." In a poem called
"Kräftgång," referring to the way crayfish ("kräftor") walk backwards,

the standard word "bekräfta" ("confirm") suddenly becomes crayfish-like.
Translating Berg demonstrates a paradoxical quality of the deformation
zone: that as we drill down more minutely into her language, we sense the
field of language expand.

5.

Instead of the expected birth narrative that leads to epiphanies about the
natural and authentic, Berg's book becomes a deformation zone of writing. It fulfills the threats posed in *The Phaedrus*. The one true child proliferates, becomes involved in theoretical – possibly false – scientific texts and
sci-fi texts. The foreign pollutes, but so does the "domestic," as Berg finds
a strange language of neologisms and "fat" sounds inside Swedish itself.
Perhaps the best "symbol" for this impure poetics of pollution is the figure
of the "myling" – an old Swedish folkloric ghost that comes from a baby
murdered by the mother and who reveals the site of its murder (usually a
well or a basement) through a strange song:

Myling

Barnköttsvampens sötsyrliga blekhet
Mjälla och porösa barnköttsblekhet
Den är fettvitskivlingen
Den är skuggan i skogen
av kosmiska Sascha
Den skrattande ryckningarharen

Myling

The babymeat mushroom's sweetsour paleness
Fluffwhite and porous babymeat paleness
It is the fatwhite agaric
It is the shadow in the forest
of cosmic Sascha
The laughing flinch-hare

When I re-read my translation, I wonder why I translated "fettviskivlin-
gen" as "agaric." It is the standard translation of the name "vitskivling,"
a treacherous poisonous mushroom (that is white and thus looks "pure"
and non-poisonous, it is one might say an example of art or artifice in

nature), but the Swedish word consists of a compound of the words "vit" and "skivor" (slices or folds). In English these kinds of mushrooms are sometimes called "gilled mushrooms." So I might have translated the word as "fatwhiteslices" or, to go along with the nautical theme of the book and the English usage, "fatwhitegills." I chose to retain "agaric" here because the semantic meaning of the word seems important; it seemed important that we know that it is a mushroom she is talking about. This is not just a poem of "opacity"; it is a poem in which language is both opaque and polluted by meaning, or meaningful and ruined by the "fat" of language, the material that is used to create pale, fat babies. Even in birth, there is death; in nature, there is artifice.

I can imagine translating "fettvitskivlingen" as the "fatwhitegilled mushroom" or any number of other variations. On one hand, my unorthodox use of language in translating Berg might be said to follow Philip Lewis's call for a translation practice that "values experimentation, tampers with usage, seeks to match the polyvalencies and the plurivocities or expressive stresses of the original by producing its own."[74] But my translations are not about mastering the foreign text and then reproducing its mastered essence. I am not in charge of Berg's work: it manipulates me into reading it without any illusion of fluency or mastery. Nor is the strangeness coming out of the translation: the book is already in circulation in Swedish, already immersing me in its strange language, changing me – my English but also my Swedish. In such a relationship, I am not foreignizing a text (as Venuti calls for); it is foreignizing me. And in such a deformation zone, there cannot be one perfect translation; it calls out for multiple translations (and indeed, Berg's work has been translated into many different languages – such as German and Chinese – but I could very easily imagine alternative translations into English, even back into Swedish). To read it best, I would argue, you have to read it without the illusion of mastery or fluency. An immigrant or beginning learner of Swedish might have the best understanding of this book, perhaps even better than the author herself.

6.

In her essays, Berg frequently explores the political importance of this kind of "vibribrating" poetry that is not redeemed by the bourgeois economics of the Lockean model of communication. The politics of *Transfer Fat* comes out of the way it infects and devours the boundaries of the "restricted economy" of mastery and fluency. Berg's essay "Language and Madness" gives an extensive account of the conflict between a utilitarian

[74]Qtd. in Kathleen Davis, *Deconstruction and Translation* (London: Routledge, 2014), 84.

approach to language and a "joyful babbling" of language – a language made materially intensive. Such a "vibribrating" and "harey" language "fattens" up the utilitarian, capitalist language.

In "It's Not Ok to be Fatso," Berg approaches the relationship between "fat" and "communication": "Communication in poetry is a path through one's own impossibility." Communication may be impossible, but it leads through one's own being. Poetry, Berg argues, is about getting "damaged" and subjecting oneself to "the least common version of reality." The impossibility of one's own experience of communication is located in the body. And it's not a body that is controlling; it's a body that is vulnerable, incomplete, subject to foreign influences and infections.

In the same essay, Berg makes an explicit connection between "fat" and the bad taste that the literary establishment is always trying to abject:

> I hope for poetic expressions that are aggressive, baroque and esoteric; I prefer the ridiculous or embarrassing to the perfect. On the literary market place, which has been dominated by the upper middle class's aesthetic and social ideals, it's not accepted to be a fatso in any regard whatsoever – one too many adjectives and you're gone. It's a persistent cliché that the sober, quiet and elegant, the "simple" by definition has more to say than the noisy. The fleshy, screamy and overloaded, the vulgar, desperate and pathetic are so taboo in our culture that it smells like a rat.

The "baroque" and excessive, the noisy and "aggressive" runs counter to an ideal of poetry based on economics: not too many adjectives, as Berg notes. As in Steiner's response to translation, the very idea of the literary establishment – whether in Sweden or the US – is to maintain an economic stability, both in the poem and the literary landscape, based on a model of "communication." Allowing too many words suggests a move away from communication, away from a poetry based on the "gold-standard" of meaning, toward a poetry of affect and kitsch, of "the orgy of verbomania," of the kind of immersion that spits out the sinthome, the rat of our literary culture.

7

GROTESQUE POEMS, HAUNTED TRANSLATIONS: THE BLACKENED SPACE OF KIM HYESOON AND DON MEE CHOI

"I failed to maintain distance with Pig, so at times I as too close to it as well as too far. I was sad when I was too far, and when I was too close, my body stank."[75]

---

[75]Kim Hyesoon, "Excerpted from an interview in Munyejungang," *Sorrowtoothpaste Mirrorcream*, trans. Don Mee Choi (South Bend: Action Books, 2014).

1.

In both Kim Hyesoon's poetry and Don Mee Choi's translations of Kim's poetry (and in her writing about this process), the subject – of the reader, the writer – is constantly contaminating and contaminated by the political and historical. This co-contamination opens up deformation zones in which poetry engages with political forces. Unlike the common model of the political being something that takes place among rational discussion in an idealized "public space," Kim's poetry takes place in what Choi calls a "blackened space" – an abject, feminine space, a private world that is constantly violently flooded by the systemic violence of globalist capitalism and neo-colonialism. But it is also out of this space that she enters into a deformation zone in which her poems are powerfully entangled in this violence, registering the violence in grotesque and often damaged bodies.

Kim's book *To Write as a Woman* (in David Krolikoski's translation) begins: "Perhaps the biggest reason for me to write these essays is a desire for communication." However, she is soon overwhelmed by a proliferation of questions which caused an idea to "intrude" on her: that "poetry is a feminine genre" and that this means to write while "possessed by ghosts" and "possessed by femininity." The "intrusion" of this idea into her consciousness suggests that the idea itself is a kind of haunting. This is perhaps a model of not just femininity and poetry, but of a certain mode of translation. As Lori Chamberlain has pointed out, the translator is often dismissed in gendered language as a feminine figure - lacking the power to assert the original, she merely mimics the original. It is perhaps because

of this intersection of gender, poetry and translation that Don Mee Choi
has argued that Kim's poetry is a "poetry of translation." This is so not because it ignores the conflicts and violent erotic imbalances of transgressive
circulation, but because it is written in exactly that toxic state.

2.

In an interview with Ruth Williams, Kim Hyesoon gives this account of
how she became a poet:

> As a sick kid, I always looked out the window. The objects of my
> observation were the sun, the seasons, the wind, crazy people, and
> my grandfather's death. During my long period of observation, I
> felt that something like poems were filling up my body. They were
> in some kind of state and condition that made them difficult to
> render into words. As a university student, I tried hard to write
> them in Korean. It was at that time that I foresaw my death and
> the world's death. I think my poems started at that time.[76]

Kim entered poetry by being moved out of official culture, into a sick
room—a space of isolation, of childhood—and she began to experience
poetry in an altered state, when her sick and radically open body began
to "fill up" with poetry—from the outside. This sense of boundaries and
borders constantly overflowing is a key trope in Kim's poetry. It's not a lib-
eratory paradigm: the contamination doesn't lead her to triumph over the
world—instead she foresees her own death "and the world's death"—but
she is not afraid of dying, not afraid of her subjecthood being ruined or
her body getting contaminated. Rather, there's a recognition that poetry
both comes out of and participates in this overflowing of boundaries.

Kim explores the poetics and politics of this kind of porous vulnerability
in her critical writing on what she calls "Princess Abandoned," drawing on
a Korean tale of the "seventh daughter," or "Paridegi," who is abandoned
by her parents for being female. Kim compares the poet to the lot of the
seventh daughter: she is made invisible, or enters a zone of "death that is
alive," but it's exactly this marginalized state that allows her to be a poet.
The key to becoming "the performer of the Abandoned" (which is what
Kim describes as her model of a certain kind of poet) is to

> ... have the experience of hearing the spirits of the dead who are
> called ghosts, spirits, or gods, in addition to having the experi-

---

[76]Kim Hyesoon, "The Female Grotesque," *Guernica* (1 January 2012), https://www.guernicamag.com/williams_kim_1_1_12/.

ence of going through a penance within a life of ordeal, suffering from shaman-sickness, or undergoing with her own body a world of illusions.[77]

Kim's poet dwells in an underworld, on the margins. She describes this space as "something closed, something black. Eyes are closed, so everything is black. It refers to being in a state of death."[78] Unlike the space of legitimacy, this is a space of abjection. It is worth remembering here that Kim Hyesoon is a founder of Korea's feminist Another Culture movement, a movement of resistance to the sexist, patriarchal and militaristic elements of Korean culture, informed in part by French theorists such as Kristeva and Cixous. With its roots in both feminist theory and the Korean folktale of the seventh daughter, Kim's figure of the poet is always feminine. She valorizes the feminine by placing her emphasis on the disempowered, subjected, abandoned element in society, and finding the root of poetry there, in resistance to a masculinized and exclusive literary and national cultures.

Kim's sense of the feminine is not concerned with biological sex; instead the feminine is a state of receptivity, defined by inclusiveness. The feminine becomes a site where all voices are heard. Specifically, this feminine, abandoned and abject state allows the poet to hear the voices of the dead, to be invaded by foreign influence, infected by the injustices of our world. In Kim's deeply immersive writing, the body is not something that corrupts the soul, or something that the mind writes about; poetry comes through the pain inflicted on the body. Unlike Augustine's binary, the body doesn't corrupt the message or meaning; the corruption or violence exerted on the body is the source of poetry. Returning to the model of communication, Kim's poetry does not come from her interiority, rather the poetic act begins by becoming invaded by ghosts, by death. The poet is haunted by this "contact." Rather than the official kind of communication Peters favors in order to create a productive society, Kim's communication acts flood her, infect her, corrupt her. There is no "interiority" separable from or unaffected by the violent mediation of poetry.

Kim's description of her poetry as communicating with the dead – or making eye-contact with a woman falling to her death – recalls an alternative side of communication that Peters discusses: the occult communication of "spiritualism." Kim shares certain features of this mode of communication: the poet is sensitive to the dead, becoming a medium for them. However, unlike the spiritualists that Peters discusses, Kim is not interested

---

[77]Kim Hyesoon, *Princess Abandoned*, trans. Don Mee Choi (Kaneohe, HI: Tinfish Press, 2012), n.p.

[78]Ibid.

in the communication between interiorities. By communicating with the dead, the poet comes in "contact" not with the feelings and individual lives of the dead so much as the "injustice" of their deaths. The poet "hears the spirits of the dead who have met unjust deaths and then intermixes the spheres of life and death."[79] The poet does not hear about the spirits' love lives or their childhood memories, but is rather possessed by the social and political violations that led to their deaths. Unlike the spiritualism that seeks to make contact with dead interiorities, Kim's poetry creates an intensive zone in which the affect saturates and overwhelms, spilling into and out of an entire landscape.

While passivity or vulnerability is often considered apolitical in our literary culture —and almost always negative – for Kim Hyesoon, this passivity becomes a politically charged position to inhabit. In her interview with Williams she notes:

> I think that solely through a language of poetry that has schizophrenia can women force the father language down from power. It is only possible with poetry to find a new Korean word or coin new Korean words. What other things can stand against it when it is a language that is a prison of discrimination for women? The language of poetry is on the margins, and it is passive, feminine, and dirty. Poetry is something that disturbs the mainstream with minor things and it is something that breaks down active discrimination with passive things, and it can break down something that polishes the filthy things with filthy things.[80]

Kim's idea of poetry as a kind of "filthy thing" invokes Kristeva's Douglas-inspired model of abjection and "pollution" (the "disturbs" here echoes Kristeva's definition of the abject as that which "disturbs" boundaries) and if it is through the poet's vulnerability (or passivity) that she becomes filled, polluted, influenced, then this is also how she commits acts of aggression against "the father language," which she pushes "down from power." We can see this as a politics of corruption – of the self, the social order, and language itself. Just as the poet is corrupted by the voices of the dead, she can corrupt the hygienic patriarchal order with her contaminated use of a "filthy" language.

---

[79]Ibid.

[80]Kim Hyesoon, "The Female Grotesque."

3.

Kim both theorizes and exemplifies this politically charged act of lan-
guage-corruption in *I'm OK, I'm Pig!*, a series of poems in which the speaker is possessed and transformed by the ghosts of pigs brutally slaughtered
to avoid contamination of the international beef trade. Kim creates an
experience that keeps collapsing the distinctions between inner/outer but
also between the poet and the speaker, and the poet and the reader, in a
filthy deformation zone of pigs and torture. Kim becomes possessed by
violently foreign entities that have been killed in order to keep out foreign
contamination. Rather than distancing herself from this "filth," she opens
herself up to contact with it. Possession, violence, invasion: The "speaker"
in these poems is constantly at "risk," constantly – often violently - changing, often addressing herself, attacking herself, auto-mutilating. Faced by
the torturous mistreatment of pigs[81], the speaker of the poem tries to med-
itate, but instead of finding solace or calmness she is invaded by the ghosts
of the dead pigs:

> Anyway, to nail Pig on a cross would be too natural, meaningless.

> I enter the Zen room, sit cross-legged and stare at the wall in order
> to meditate.

> You know, I'm confessing right now, I'm actually Pig. You know,
> I've been Pig since birth. Filthy, I'm filthy, really filthy. A mind? I
> have no such thing.

Although it is supposedly a "confession," the poem doesn't lead to the
"communication" of Kim's human "interiority." Rather, the confessing act
puts her in contact with ghosts – specifically the non-human pigs that have
been mass-slaughtered to prevent contamination. Instead of revealing her
interiority, she herself is transformed into "pig," made "filthy" – even in
a meditation room – with the ghosts of global capitalism, rupturing the
containment of this space. She both becomes a pig and fights against the
pigs. In short, the Zen room that was meant to lead to calmness becomes
the site where the pigs – emblems of corporality, "filth" and violence – and
the speaker enter into a deformation zone with the systemic violence of
global capitalism.

---

[81]In an interview with Munyejungung, Kim explains the origins of the poem: "As you know, last year, three million pigs were buried
due to the outbreak of foot-and-mouth disease in our country. And countless numbers of cows were also buried. Almost all of the cows
and pigs in South Korea went into the ground. Their pink bodies, whether they were diseased or about to be diseased, were difficult to
dispose of, so they were buried alive" (Kim Hyesoon,"Excerpt from an interview in *Munyejungang*").

This state of transgressive circulation is not an act of "communication" and it is far from peaceful. Repeatedly throughout the suite, the pigs reject her act of communion with them. In "Your Imperial Majesty, Ferroconcrete!" the speaker – as poet, as pig, as observer of herself as poet – engages in a furious argument with herself:

> Where do you want me to go?
> Who the hell are you?
> Why do you write?
> Are you saying you want to get killed right now?
> Or are you telling me to die?
> You jerk who live on the suffering of others

In these lines, it is as if the speaker/author interrogates herself about her act of channeling the dead pigs. This interrogation seems to lead to confusion: "Who the hell are you?" she asks herself. In a sense the "I" of the poem becomes the "you" here; in the moment she separates herself from the pigzone, she becomes a "you," incomprehensible to herself. The poem at this point seems written from the point of view of the pig-zone, where there can be no coherent "I." Arthur Rimbaud's classic statement "Je est un autre" becomes hyperbolic and atrocious.

The pigzone is not a space for balanced "exchange," the kind Steiner and Locke are so concerned about. It's an excessive zone of proliferation, a space of eating and being eaten, of attacking and being attacked, of abjection and violence: "I'm filthy, really filthy." Everybody attacks everybody else; it is not clear who is whom or who is killing whom. This is a zone of what Joyelle McSweeney has called "ambient violence": "It's relatively easy to process violent poetry when it presents a critique of violence. But what about when ambient violence makes a medium of a body and makes it a perpetrator of violence against itself and others?"[82] There is no transcendence in this world, no escape from this violence: "Anyway to nail Pig on a cross would be too natural, meaningless." The poems announce that symbolism won't work in this world. Even Marilyn Monroe, American icon of beauty and glamour, is brought into the pig-sphere. Monroe may once have "lived in a world as pure as the movie screen" but now her ghosts speaks: "We return as pigs/We snap back onto the pig magnet that eats and shits." As in Kristeva's theory of abjection, the filth returns.

---

[82]Joyelle McSweeney, "A New Quarantine Will Take My Place, or, Ambient Violence, or, Bringing it All Back Home," *Montevidayo* (11 Oct. 2010), http://montevidayo.com/2010/10/a-new-quarantine-will-take-my-place-or-ambient-violence-or-bringing-it-all-back-home/.

If there is a heart of this sequence, it may be the prose piece "Pig Pigs Out." In this poem, the pigs "pig out" – through birth, slaughter or art. Early in the poem "mommy [gives] birth to Pig who will pig out till it drops dead." Giving birth begins this constant self-immolating process of "pigging out": self-perpetuating the piggery. The piggery enters the very language of the poem: "whenever it opens its mouth makes pig pig sounds Pig pork Pig." The constant repetition of pig accumulates an excess of pig-ness: there are no individual pigs, they are also sounds, even when those sounds are broken down into butchered "pork." This line is followed by a series of lines that begins "qqqq." This is the "sound of pig," but it's also a translation noise: the repetition of a Korean consonant with no direct relationship to the English alphabet.[83] The pigs become a volatile materi-ality of language – a radical corruption of interiority or meaning that is exaggerated when Choi translated these pig-sounds into English.

Pigs watching pigs. Pigs making art about pigs. Pigs making pigs out of pigs. Pigs "pigging out": a self-collapsing act of making pigs, of being a pig, physically embodying the pig. The verb is so physical, so piggish that it cannot redeem the "stuff" of the pig, the "fat" of the pig (in Berg's words), rejecting any conceptual standard that would redeem it. In this inflation-ary zone of pig-transformations, language itself becomes pig-ish: saturat-ed, thick and neologistic, as if the poem was pushing the words together, squeezing language into an onomatopoeic mess.

In Choi's translation, the English language becomes denaturalized and de-formed: "qqqq, most of all the squeals of nation's pigs that don't know that I'm Pig." But at the same time, it never seems distancing, pedagogic as in the experimental or academic model, but rather it becomes increasingly overwhelming, absorbing: "Plates-break oil-splatter soy-sauce-pours-out I'm-tired my-wrist-gets-scalded." Like the poet, readers are drawn into the atrocious deformation zone where the English language becomes infected by the Korean, by the myriad of pigs that global capitalism sickened and then murdered. Even the English language itself cannot be kept clean of these atrocities.

4.

It is important that in Kim's poetry it is the body – wounded, excessive, proliferating, eating and eaten, violent and violated, abject and abjecting – that registers the political violence of neocolonialism, global capitalism

---

[83]Email from Don Mee Choi, Sunday Nov 23, 2014: yes it is just a sound. qqqq is ㅋㅋㅋㅋ in Korean. It's a Korean alphabet (conso-nant). Letter q in english sounded the closest to ㅋ so that's why we decided on q.

and patriarchal mores. It is important that even the language – with its excessive qqqq-sounds and syntactic "pigging out" –becomes bodily and grotesque. On one hand this is simply because this systemic violence registers very visibly on bodies (women's bodies, pigs, children). But it is also, I would argue, because Kim's poetry itself enacts a violence against the private, the interior, the secluded through transgressive circulation. It makes sense that the result is a grotesque poetics. In *On Longing*, Susan Stewart describes how the miniature (often represented by the dollhouse) becomes the model for bourgeois interiority, while the grotesque—with its exaggeration and discombobulated body parts— comes to signify the ruination of that private space. Stewart notes:

> The miniature world remains perfect and uncontaminated by the grotesque as long as the absolute boundaries are maintained... The glass eliminates the possibility of contagion, indeed of lived experience, at the same time that it maximizes the possibilities of transcendent vision.[84]

However, Stewart also recognizes that:

> ...the major function of the enclosed space is always to create a tension or dialectical between inside and outside, between private and public property, between the space of the subject and the space of the social.[85]

Kim Hyesoon's poems frequently take place in a miniature world, a private space – such as the Zen mediation room, but more frequently simply a room or a box or a house– that is overwhelmed, ruined by contagion or trespass, flood or sheer violence. The "social" inevitably explodes or seeps through the perfect glass wall. Kim creates miniatures in order to stage this tension between the private and public, a tension that more often than not results in rupture and contamination.

What happens when this containment is broken? Stewart discusses the role of the body in attempting to make sense of the melee of the world (outside the miniature's perfect realm):

> When the body is the primary mode of perceiving scale, exaggeration must take place in relation to the balance of measurement offered as the body extends into the space of immediate experience. But paradoxically, the body itself is necessarily exaggerated

---

[84]Susan Stewart, *On Longing: Narratives of the Miniature, the Gigantic, the Souvenir, the Collection* (Durham: Duke U.P., 1984), 68.
[85]Ibid., 68.

> as soon as we have an image of the body, an image which is a projection or objectification of the body into the world. Thus the problems in imagining the body are symptomatic of the problems in imagining the self as place, object, and agent at once[86]

Kim's poetry often takes place in this vertiginous zone of the body: exploring its many shifts in scale, she explores what it is like to have a body in the world, what it is like to make art with this body in a social sphere where that body is never quite the authenticity-granting foundation of so many models of the body, but rather is overrun with the social and necessarily distorted through the imagining of the body. Kim's grotesque bodies are not just registering systemic political violence, they are also registering the problems of "imagining the self as a place, object, and agent."

5.

As with the work of Aase Berg, the question becomes: How does one translate this kind of corrosively corrupted, overwhelming, grotesque poetry? How does one engage with a poetry that stages the problems of "imagining the self as a place"? How do we as Americans interact with poetry from South Korea, a country which the US has subjected to massive amounts of colonial and neocolonial violence, a country where the US has backed a series of totalitarian dictatorships and brutally capitalist regimes, a country which the US is still inflicting violence on (such as the massive destruction of the beautiful and culturally important Jeju Island for the purpose of building a US navy base)? This is especially important to consider in the case of a poet like Kim, whose work frequently addresses the very injustices and brutalities brought on or back up by US support.

Venuti might say that it's the translator's job to "foreignize" the poems to thus call attention to the historical inequalities and violent acts that separate the US from South Korea. I would argue that such an approach to translation would be self-contradictory: it would contradict the immersive, visceral poetics of Kim's poetry in order to make its historical position clear and tastefully distant for the US reader. Further, while it's true that American readers will not have the same background as Korean readers, I think the questions above actually suggest the way we are in fact part of the same cultural context: US imperialism and global capitalism has made Korea part of the US political and cultural hegemony. Don Mee Choi's visceral, powerful translations of Kim's work counter this hegemony by making US readers part of Korean poetry, part of a poetry that bears

---

[86]Ibid., 132.

the scars of US hegemony. That is to say, the translations aim to ruin the private spaces US citizens have built for themselves while US military and economic forces have brutalized the rest of the world.

Don Mee Choi's translations will not overcome the political inequalities of the US and Korea. Like Kim's poetry, her translations will engage with them, staging the violence as a perpetual zone of "ambient violence." Critics who want translation to be an act of "communication," an act of finding the "accurate equivalent," necessarily depoliticize the act of translation and erase difference; translation critics often emphasize the "untranslatability" of texts, arguing that it is impossible for texts to cross cultural boundaries, but Choi and Kim show how those borders are porous and, though there are important cultural and political differences (for example between Korea and the US), this doesn't mean the translations become impossible. Instead, the translations become absolutely necessary.

In her introduction to *Mommy Must Be A Fountain of Feathers*, the first single-volume collection of Kim Hyesoon's work published in English, Choi writes that Kim writes out of the "blackened space" of writing censored by the Korean government: "For Kim the blackened space is not only the space of oppression but also a place where a woman redefines herself, retranslates herself. Therefore, I see Kim's poetry as poetry of translation." It is exactly in the "invisibility" of marginalization and oppression that Kim finds her poetry, and this is a poetry of translation, coming out of an invisible, illegitimate space similar to the one Venuti ascribes to the "invisibility of translation." But contrary to Venuti, Kim's poetry is not about becoming "visible" and legitimate, working within the strictures of society, but to bring the obscene "blackened space" into visibility, to corrupt the "father language" with her "filthy" poetry. Choi describes her translation as engaged with a similar act, out of the same blackened space:

> And in my role as a translator, I guide Kim's translated blackened self to another place, another language, across a bridge forged by history – the history of the US presence in Korea since 1945. The US presence translates into about one hundred US military bases and installations in South Korea, a land that is only one fourth the size of California... I need to state the obvious: South Korean is a neocolony.[87]

Choi's translation is not the attempt to "recreate" an "original," but to bring it – its blackened, obscene vision, its "sheer stuff," its kitsch, its "filthy

---

[87]*Mommy Must Be a Fountain of Feathers*, 9.

things," its "fat," its wounds, its grotesque body and language – across the bridge built by colonial politics and global economics between Korean and English.

In this gothic vision of poetry and translation, Kim and Choi become uncanny doubles, "two daughters too many," an excess.[88] Choi recounts that when Kim was asked how she felt about being translated, Kim replied, "It's like meeting someone like myself."[89] The blackened realm of poetry generates doubles, too-much-ness. In the blackened space where poetry is translation and vice versa, Choi "dwells" in Kim's "house," that constantly ruptured space where the I tries and fails to imagine itself as a space, that space that cannot keep out history's political violence. And because poem and translation dwell in the same blackened space, the translation "exists on the same plane as the original poem," not as an inferior (or superior) version. In this gothic doubling, Kim and Choi undo the traditional model of the translator as the US expert who masters a foreign culture and brings back a flawed attempt to recreate an original. Choi's and Kim's relationship is much more visceral, volatile.

Unlike translation advocates such as Venuti, who insists on making translators legitimate, Choi insists on the translator's lowliness, her "failure," her abjectness. In "Freely Frayed+=q + Race =Nation," she writes: "It turns out that I'm a mere imitator, the lowly kind, which is none other than a translator, a mimicker of mimetic words… I twirl about frantically frequently farfar to the point of failure feigning englishenglish." Choi positions the translator as a failure – for example a failure to properly master the Korean with masterful English, leading to "englishenglish" instead of "English" - but it's exactly in this failure that the strength of her translations, as well as Kim's originals, comes from. Choi writes: "translation is a process of perpetual displacement." She writes:

> The displaced poetic identity persists in its dislocation, translating itself out of the orders of darkness through the translator, another displaced identity. We have no choice but failfail. Failingfailing, it's painful becoming a translation, becoming an immigrant.[90]

Choi participates in Kim's transgressive circulation, a circulation that ruins the private space, the clean space of patriarchy. As she does, she suffers from exactly the kind of "foreign influence" Steiner fears: the foreign language corrupts and disables her, causing her to become a "failingfailing"

[88]Ibid., 10.

[89] Qtd. in Joyelle McSweeney, *The Necropastoral: Poetry, Media, Occults* (Ann Arbor: University of Michigan Press, 2012), 66.

[90]Don Mee Choi, "On Kim Hyesoon's *Mommy Must Be A Fountain of Feathers*," *Essay Press* #22, 6.

translator – both invisible and hypervisible like the "blackened space" of Kim Hyesoon's poetry.

If Kim's poetry is a translation-based poetry – a poetry of transgressive circulation – then so are Choi's translations of Kim's poems: they "failfail" by contaminating the English language with the qqqq-stutters of the Kim's Korean. As with Aase Berg's poetry, we can see in both Kim and Choi what Gilles Deleuze and Felix Guattari understood as the politics of a "minor" language. Not to be confused with (though not necessarily totally divorced from) minority literature, minor literature is a kind of "revolutionary" literature that undermines the stability of languages from within: "There is nothing that is major or revolutionary except the minor. To hate all languages of masters... be a stranger within one's own language."[91] Choi's "failingfailing" English is an English deterritorialized by the foreign Korean language. Her translations become the deformation zone where English is contaminated by the minor.

By pushing Kim's Korean through the English language, Choi's translations commit violence to the "master language" of English. The result is a "materially intense," "physicalized" language, as Deleuze and Guattari would have it, and as we have seen in Aase Berg's poetry. Because the signification-function is short-circuited, minor literature emphasizes the physical aspect of language. Choi's qqqq-ing of the English is akin to Kafka's deterritorialization of German through Gregor Samsa's buzzing. In Deleuze and Guattari's theories of "minor literature," we can see the political valence of both Kim's poems and Choi's translations of those poems.

7.

In one of her essays on translating Kim's work, Choi compares Kim's poetry to Shohei Imamura's film *Pigs and Battleship* (1961), in which pigs are let loose in the city of Yokosuka, bewildering the US GIs:

> ...when Imamura says he wanted to show the "power of pigs" by releasing hundreds of pigs into the GI streets of Yokosuka, the pigs become powerful pigs. They fill every alley, crushing everything in their way, and the thugs who have eaten the pigs are pigs, and the women in prostitution who prepare pigs for their Japanese male customers and GIs and eat pigs are also pigs. Yokosuka becomes a pig town. Kim's and Imamura's animals both instruct us how to subvert the order of power.[92]

---

[91] Deleuze and Guattari, *Kafka: Toward a Minor Literature*, 26.
[92] Don Mee Choi, "On Kim Hyesoon's *Mommy Must Be A Fountain of Feathers*," 4.

For Choi, these repulsive, sick animals and this movie become emblems for a poetry of subversion, but the pigs could also be read as an allegory for the way translation's failure to properly communicate interiority takes on a social, political dimension. The streets of Yokosaka, convulsing with pigs, are like the channels of abject and violent communication. Convulsing with pigs, Yokosuka becomes much like the "Seoul" of Kim's poems (in Choi's description): "Everything in its landscape enters and exits Seoul. Hence Seoul is always in the flux of becoming itself." The poems, the film and "Seoul": all participate in a deformation zone convulsed by transgressive circulation. It is in the space of the poem, what Kim calls a "performance space," where poet and reader can listen to, even become possessed by the dead, and thus to recognize the "injustice" of their lives. In each regard, the abjectness becomes key to a poetry that is political and convulsive.

Choi's translation is not an attempt to recrcate a pristine original, so much as to bring the blackened, "filthy" vision – the materially saturated and saturating poetry – into view. In Choi's model there is none of the idyllic idea of "exchange," an economic model, which, as we have seen, hides a conservative idea based on stable ideas of context and tradition: Kim's poetry is already in circulation because the world is in circulation (sometimes horrifically). Choi herself – as an immigrant, as a translator – does not belong to a stable idea of "American Literature," but functions as a weak spot, a site of infection, which shows that there is no such thing as a national literature, only an illusion maintained by the people who benefit from this monoglossic ideal.

The translator is "invisible" because the US literary culture is invested in mastery and centrality, a monoglossic dynamic that participates in US hegemony abroad and the marginalization of difference cultural and aesthetic groups at home. It's exactly in its abject status that translation is the most powerful, most transgressive: when it threatens not just reductive models of national literatures, but also authoritative models of authorship. I think the greatest poetry – and the most important translations – are not written by "visible" and respectable figures who expose our illusions for us, but by writers and translators who make that invisibility materially intensive, bringing a "blackened space" to readers. As Venuti points out, American cultural imperialism goes hand in hand with economic and military imperialism: instead of making the ghosts hygienic, we must become infected by them, we must become "Pig," taken over by their transgressive circulation.

8

CONCLUSION

1.

People from around the world have no choice: they are constantly translating texts (and songs, films, news). Indeed, people around the US have no choice: immigrants are constantly translating in order to survive. Only in a hegemonic center – held up by money, laws and military strength – can people act as if they don't need to read foreign literature. The connection may seem extreme, but as Lawerence Venuti, Eric Bennet and Richard So Jean have shown: poetry is not isolated from imperialism and global political movements. This should give us some pause, but it should also give us inspiration: poetry is not apolitical, not pointless or without effect. We help create the language which holds together our nation, and so we can also make language more elastic, more vulnerable to foreign influence, more welcoming of diversity and volatile movements.

2.

Our literary culture is still highly centripetal – focused on maintaining order, centrality, hierarchy. Even if one turns one's attention to social media and Twitter, one sees a paradoxical double movement: on the one hand, new and lawless networks among writers and readers of various economic and national statuses seem to form before one's eyes, while on another, one sees a tendency to tweet and re-tweet prize, fellowship, residency, and book contract announcements. Visibility is the vindication of the marginalized, but a visibility which always seems to shore up extant centers of literary power runs the risk of neutralizing the anti-hegemonic force of minor literature. As such, mainstream literary culture participates in a larger politics of US hegemony abroad and erasure or co-optation of various cultural and aesthetic groups at home. Translation has the potential to trouble this dynamic. With its occult and illimitable volatility, translation troubles borders and hierarchies, making US poetry vulnerable not only to foreign movements and authors but also to multiplicities and movements within the US.

3.

Mainstream US literary culture still revolves around the idea of the great author, the Chosen One with the "talent" (to quote T.S. Eliot) of rendering their inner vision to others in great feats of communication. Such talent is usually made to appear self-evident via residencies, grants, contracts, etc, -- self-confirming cycles of reward that represent a constricted and limited poetic ecosystem. Yet this role of consensus in creating the spectre of the 'great poet' is generally hidden behind the ideology of the 'individual talent'. Translation brings in alternative canons and texts, and in so doing it also opens up alternative models of authorship. Rather than the singular great author, translation foregrounds the collaborative element of writing as well as the cultural issues and contexts at play in both the creation and transmission of the text.

4.

A poetry that is profoundly engaged with foreign poetry is a poetry that is aware that nations are not homogenous, that while the institutions of literature are almost always hierarchical, writing itself is not. One frequently heard standard for translation is that the translation should read as it would read to a speaker in the native country. But this criterion makes it seem as if the readers in the original country are all the same, all with the same interpretations and reading approaches. Further, it makes it seem like poems are always written for the most educated (which tends to mean richest, most privileged) readers. As I suggested in the chapter on Aase Berg, I want to suggest that poetry is not always – or even mostly – written for some kind of elite class of readers and writers with the proper learning and – thus – taste. Poetry may be written for and by immigrants and emigrants, for and by weirdos, for and by readers with strange or unusual reading habits, for and by people who read via transnational contexts, for and by people who have no desire or ability to "master" the poem. Poetry, I have argued, is at its strongest when we don't have the crutches of mastery; when we are thrown into its deformation zone.

5.

Translation can of course be used conservatively. We see this in the creation of a canon of foreign writers, whose work is continually – and absurdly – held up as representative of entire literatures, re-translated and written about while newer poets are ignored. This work has been approved and accepted, thus removing the stain and suspicion of translation: the establishment can trust that it is quality literature, that it has been properly translated. This work is portrayed as somehow rising above its national boundaries, sometimes imagined as a 'Republic of Letters'. This work is "good" because it can be translated; that is to say, because it is not affected by the translation. We can also see this conservatism in the repeated re-translation of this same canon of foreign poets (Federico Garcia Lorca, Pablo Neruda, Rilke, Thomas Tranströmer), great poets who at one point had a transformative effect on US poetry but whose repeated canonization has now become conservative, a barrier against engagement with new (whether contemporary or older) poets with deregulatory potential.

6.

Rather than raise foreign poets above their national boundaries, I suggest we keep the boundaries in mind, pay attention to what they do to the poems, but nonetheless allow ourselves to be fully put under the influence of these foreign works. That is to say, neither to ignore their foreignness nor exoticize or "foreignize" their foreignness, but enter into their poetry's deformation zone.

7.

In conversation, some have said to me that they have nothing against translation, they simply haven't found a foreign poet they like yet. Or they may say: I would love to read foreign literature but translation simply isn't the real thing. Both cases reflect a model of poetry that in fact excludes translation, excludes the foreign. Whether overt or not, such stances follow Frost's claim that poetry is what is "lost in translation." And if one's definition excludes foreign poetry, one must either accept that one has a fundamentally xenophobic view of poetry, or one can change one's view of poetry in order to open it up to the foreign.

8.

As I have argued throughout this provocation, opening up one's view to the deregulatory capacity of poetry in translation is not extraneous to poetry, it is at the heart of poetry. The reason I spend so much time discussing objections to translation is that in these objections I see attempts not just to exclude translation, but to limit the power of poetry, to bring it into an elitist economy of restraint. By opening up to poetry in translation – by piercing the boundaries between the "nearly-baroque" and the "neo-baroque" – we not only find a new style, we can create a more volatile US poetry. To create such volatility, we must read foreign poetry and bring foreign poetries into US poetry discussions, but we must also allow this foreign poetry to make US poetry foreign to ourselves. Poetry in translation has the capacity of not just being assimilated by US poetry, but of finding in US poetry not just one homogenous, hierarchical US poetry, but a myriad of US poetries.

9.

Such a centrifugal myriad of poetries is of course a nightmare to critics and poets who want there to be a defined US poetry that they can know, evaluate and master. But poetry is not meant to be mastered. It is meant to draw us into its foreign orbits, its circulation.

ACKNOWLEDGEMENTS

Some of these essays have appeared in different versions in several journals and websites, including *Med Andra Ord*, Asian-American Writers Workshop, *Denver Quarterly*, *Cordite Poetry Review*, *The Volta*, *Montevidayo*, *Nypoesi*, and *Boston Review*. They've also been given as talks and lectures at ALTA, Saas-Fee Summer Institute of Art in Berlin, Illinois State University, Oxford University, MLA, ASAP Conference, AWP Conference, Indiana University, ACLA, &Now Conference, and Helsinki Poetics Conference. An early version of my thesis was published as a booklet, *The Deformation Zone* (with Joyelle McSweeney, Ugly Duckling Presse). Thanks to the generosity of all the organizers and editors of these sites and publications.

Thanks also to many translators, critics, poets and friends with whom I've discussed ideas about translation and/or versions of this book: Daniel Borzutzky, Don Mee Choi, Katherine Hedeen, Molly Weigl, Jeffrey Angles, Christian Hawkey, Aase Berg, Clemens Altgård, Lucas Klein, Daniel Tiffany, Kate Marshall, Steve Fredman, Douglas Robinson, Lawrence Venuti, Jiyoon Lee, Matvei Yankelevich, Anna Moschavakis, Lara Glenum, Josef Horáček, Sara Tuss Efrik, Jed Rasula, and my students at the University of Notre Dame.

Thanks as well to Emily Alex for her skilled editing of the manuscript.

Most of all thanks to Joyelle McSweeney for the constant conversations, ideas and inspirations.